DAVID W. OWENS

CONFLICTS
of
INTEREST
in
Land-Use Management Decisions

1990

INSTITUTE OF GOVERNMENT
THE UNIVERSITY OF NORTH CAROLINA AT CHAPEL HILL

THE INSTITUTE OF GOVERNMENT of The University of North Carolina at Chapel Hill is devoted to teaching, research, and consultation in state and local government.

Since 1931 the Institute has conducted schools and short courses for city, county, and state officials. Through monographs, guidebooks, bulletins, and periodicals, the research findings of the Institute are made available to public officials throughout the state.

Each day that the General Assembly is in session, the Institute's *Daily Bulletin* reports on the Assembly's activities for members of the legislature and other state and local officials who need to follow the course of legislation.

Over the years the Institute has served as the research agency for numerous study commissions of the state and local governments.

John L. Sanders, DIRECTOR
William A. Campbell, ASSOCIATE DIRECTOR

FACULTY

Contents

CHAPTER ONE

Introduction

It is clear that a city council member should not vote on rezoning his own property. But what about rezoning the property next door? Should a county commissioner vote on a proposed subdivision that would adjoin her own neighborhood, affecting traffic, services, and perhaps her own property's value? What about a city council member voting on a special-use permit for a project when his employer has a contract to furnish the building materials if the project is approved? Although a member of a zoning board of adjustment should not vote on her own variance request, what if the request is being made by her son? What if her son is the petitioner's realtor? What about voting on a project against which the member signed a petition before being appointed to the board of adjustment? Does a different rule apply when planning commission members are making a recommendation than when they are rendering a final decision?

When land-use management programs are being developed and administered, decisions are made that significantly affect both the community at large and individuals. These decisions require the exercise of judgment and discretion. They frequently involve basic choices about governmental policies. Therefore an effort has been made to put as many of these decisions as possible directly in the hands of citizens. Citizen boards, not professional staff members or judges, adopt ordinances and regulations, issue special-use permits, and grant variances.

The author is an Institute faculty member specializing in land-use and natural resource law. An abbreviated nonlegal version of this book was previously published by the Institute of Government as Owens, *Bias and Conflict of Interest in Land-Use Management Decisions*, 55 POPULAR GOV'T 29 (Winter 1990).

Because of the importance of these decisions, there is a strong public interest in securing knowledgeable citizens to serve on the many citizen boards involved in the land-use process—planning boards, boards of adjustment, city councils, county boards, and state regulatory commissions. Yet these same knowledgeable citizens are also likely to be personally involved in land development and in neighborhood and environmental groups. They may make their livings as builders, realtors, surveyors, or bankers. They may have organized neighborhood associations or led groups favoring or opposing controversial development projects. In sum, their knowledge and wisdom often come from experience—their active personal participation in land-use issues.

Therein lies an inherent tension. Although government needs the participation of knowledgeable citizens, it also is obligated to provide fair and unbiased decisions, giving equal treatment to all. Citizens have the right to expect that governmental decisions will be based on consideration of what is in the best public interest, not what will most benefit the personal finances or concerns of an individual citizen board member. This right is based on constitutional guarantees of due process,[1] on common law principles, and on statutes, ordinances, and codes

---

1.   Withrow v. Larkin, 421 U.S. 35 (1975); Gibson v. Berryhill, 411 U.S. 564 (1973); Goldberg v. Kelly, 397 U.S. 254 (1970); *In re* Murchison, 349 U.S. 133 (1955); and Tumey v. Ohio, 273 U.S. 510 (1923). As stated by Justice Black in *Murchison,*

> A fair trial in a fair tribunal is a basic requirement of due process. Fairness of course requires an absence of actual bias . . . . But our system of law has always endeavored to prevent even the probability of unfairness. To this end no man can be a judge in his own case and no man is permitted to try cases where he has an interest in the outcome.
> [349 U.S. 133 at 136.]

For a historical review of the development of conflict-of-interest law in the United States, see Assoc. of the Bar of the City of New York, Special Committee on the Federal Conflict of Interest Laws, Conflict of Interest and Federal Service 28–59 (1960). This well-researched and thoughtful document was influential in the development of the first comprehensive federal legislation on conflicts of interest in the early 1960s. For additional background, see R. Getz, Congressional Ethics: The Conflict of Interest Issue (1966); Note, *Disqualification of Judges for Prejudice or Bias—Common Law Evolution, Current Status, and the Oregon Experience,* 48 Or. L. Rev. 311 (1969); Law School, University of Chicago, Conference on Conflict of Interest (Conference Series No. 17, 1961); National Municipal League, Model State Conflict of Interest and Financial Disclosure Law (1979). For an instructive review of the law in the British context, see S. Williams, Conflict of Interest: The Ethical Dilemma in Politics (1985). For the Canadian law, see Rogers, *Conflicts of Interest—A Trap for Unwary Politicians,* 11 Osgoode Hall L.J. 537 (1973).

On the concept of public office as a public trust, see Lenhoff, *The Constructive Trust as a Remedy for Corruption in Public Office,* 54 Colum. L. Rev. 214 (1954); Note, *The*

of conduct mandating ethics in government. Public confidence in government depends on the integrity of governmental decisions, and the attempt represented by these various forms of law to avoid bias and conflicts of interest is no doubt a factor in establishing that confidence.

Several states have adopted legislation to guide citizen board members in meeting their ethical and legal responsibility to avoid improper bias and conflict of interest in land-use decision making. Other states have had extensive litigation on this issue. North Carolina has neither adopted legislation nor had extensive litigation. This makes it difficult to define when a citizen board member should withdraw from participation in a land-use matter because of a conflict of interest. The issue is fraught with considerable ambiguity and uncertainty for the citizen attempting to discharge his or her responsibilities fairly and reasonably.

This book addresses how the tension between securing the full participation of knowledgeable and experienced citizens and securing fair and unbiased land-use decisions can be balanced in North Carolina land-use decisions.[2] This is done by looking at (1) the types of bias and conflicts of interest that arise in the land-use area, the types of land-use management decisions government makes, and the ways in which these categories affect the conflict-of-interest issue; (2) the ways in which the law has treated this subject in other states; (3) the current law on bias and conflicts of interest in North Carolina; and (4) conclusions and recommendations on how effective and active citizen involvement in land-use decision making can be secured ethically and legally. A model ordinance is presented in an appendix as a means of providing guidelines for board members in resolving conflict-of-interest questions. The key statutes, codes, and other legal provisions cited in the book are also set out in an appendix.

Federal Conflicts of Interests Statutes and the Fiduciary Principle, 14 VAND. L. REV. 1485 (1961).

    2.   Conflict of interest on the part of staff members making administrative land-use decisions is not covered directly by this book, though most of the same principles would apply. *See generally* AM. INST. OF CERTIFIED PLANNERS, ETHICAL AWARENESS IN PLANNING 23–26 (1983). For a general review of these issues from the perspective of the land-use planning profession, see Martin, *Above Reproach: A Review of the Profession's Code of Ethics*, 55 PLAN. 18 (Oct. 1989); Howe and Kaufman, *The Ethics of Contemporary American Planners*, 45 J. AM. PLAN. A. 243 (1979); Kaufman, *Ethics and Planning: Some Insights from the Outside*, 47 J. AM. PLAN. A. 198 (1981); Levin, *The Conscience of the Planner*, 42 PLAN. 8 (Jan. 1976); and McCahill, *Stealing: A Primer on Zoning Corruption*, 39 PLAN. 6 (Dec. 1973). For a discussion from the government employee's viewpoint, see A. NEELY, ETHICS-IN-GOVERNMENT LAWS: ARE THEY TOO "ETHICAL"? (1984). For a focus on attorneys, see Note, *Developments in the Law—Conflicts of Interest in the Legal Profession*, 94 HARV. L. REV. 1244 (1981).

    For a more general review of the issues involved, see K. DENHARDT, THE ETHICS OF PUBLIC SERVICE: RESOLVING MORAL DILEMMAS IN PUBLIC ORGANIZATIONS (1988).

CHAPTER TWO

Conflicts of Interest and Governmental Land-Use Management Decisions

Types of Conflicts of Interest

As used in this book, the term *conflicts of interest* refers to situations in which a citizen board member's duty to act in the public interest clashes with the member's inclination to advance his or her personal interest.[1] There is no requirement that the board member's action directly harm the public; rather the potential harm that could result from conflicting interests is at issue. Indeed, it has been noted that the intense public concern with conflicts of interest, often replete with references to Caesar's wife and officials beyond reproach, is a compliment to the fundamental honesty of present-day governmental decision

---

1.   Conflicts of interest are often characterized as the gray area between acceptable advocacy and unacceptable self-interest. As one observer noted, "Conflict of interest at one edge shades off into corruption and theft, at the other into representation of interests" [Long, Conflict of Interest: A Political Scientist's View, paper delivered at the Annual Meeting of the American Political Science Assoc., Washington, D.C. (September 6–9, 1962), at 6]. Public concern about conflicts of interest has as much a moral as a legal basis:

> As a nation, we like our politics neat. The heroes still wear white hats, and the villains black ones; we do not like to get them mixed up, and we decidedly do not like the players to wear gray hats. . . . In substantial measure, the American looks upon his politics as a Morality Play.
> [Manning, *The Purity Potlatch: An Essay on Conflicts of Interest, American Government, and Moral Escalation*, 24 Fed. B.J. 239, 243 (1964).]

making—that there is so little actual corruption that attention can be focused on preventing potential abuses caused by conflicts of interest.

The legitimacy of the exercise of governmental authority depends upon that power being exercised in accordance with fundamental principles of democratic representation. As a recent study on legislative ethics noted, democratic representation requires "that legislators be morally autonomous agents whose decisions are based on informed, unbiased, and uncoerced judgments."[2] Therefore the question is not whether a citizen board member with a conflict of interest can make a decision that is still in the public interest; undoubtedly many can. The question is the impact of such a potential for abuse on public confidence in the integrity of the decision.

There are several types of conflicts of interest in land-use decision making by government that can affect the impartiality of citizen board members. They include financial conflicts of interest, personal bias, and associations with those affected by a decision.

Financial conflicts of interest occur when citizen board members are in a position to benefit financially from the outcomes of particular decisions made by the board.[3] This includes both direct and indirect financial benefits. For example, conflicts of interest arise not only when a board member's own property is directly affected but also when a business owned by a member either stands to benefit from increased sales associated with someone else's new project or, conversely, stands to lose sales if a competing business receives a permit.

Personal interest on other than financial grounds also can create a conflict of interest. A board member may have had personal dealings with a petitioner that so color the member's judgment that he or she is unable to separate the prior unrelated encounter from the land-use issue at hand. Or a board member may have taken a strong public position on a proposed project that is later presented to the board for an objective decision based on the record developed at an adjudicatory hearing. The potential personal interest may not even involve the particular member. At times the member's association with an interested party

---

2. THE HASTINGS CENTER, THE ETHICS OF LEGISLATIVE LIFE 34 (1985).

3. A more direct financial conflict, and a clearly illegal one, is the straightforward bribe. Given the very large sums of money at stake in some land-use decisions, the temptations are such that blatantly criminal acts will occasionally be committed. Criminal corruption is not, however, the subject of this book. For a review of criminal activities and suggested remedies, see NATIONAL INSTITUTE OF LAW ENFORCEMENT AND CRIMINAL JUSTICE, U.S. DEPARTMENT OF JUSTICE, CORRUPTION IN LAND USE AND BUILDING REGULATION (1979). The federal law on the subject is codified at 18 U.S.C.A. ch. 11 (West Supp. 1990). For an analysis of the major revision of federal law on the subject in 1963, see Perkins, *The New Federal Conflicts-of-Interest Law*, 76 HARV. L. REV. 1113 (1963).

raises a potential problem. A close relative's or a business partner's involvement in a matter coming before the board is not uncommon. In these situations the question is whether the board member is making a decision based on the merits of the issue or based on his or her relationship with the applicant.

The concern is not only with *actual* conflicts, but with the *appearance* of impropriety—potential conflicts of interest as well as real ones. Public perception of the fairness of land-use decisions is an important element in the degree of citizen confidence in the decisions. In most cases, members of the public do not know government officials personally and have no way of independently verifying their integrity. As a practical matter, no one—not a close associate, not a judge, not a jury—can know for certain what motivated a board member to vote in a particular way. Therefore the avoidance of even the appearance of a conflict of interest is an important factor to be considered.

Types of Governmental Land-Use Management Decisions

Whether an improper conflict of interest exists and what response is appropriate depends in part on the type of land-use management decision involved. Although government makes many direct land-use decisions, such as where to build a new road, school, or sewer line, this book is concerned with governmental decisions by citizen boards and commissions that manage private land uses. These land-use decisions may be one of three types: advisory, legislative, or quasi-judicial. In many respects conflict-of-interest scrutiny increases as one progresses from advisory to legislative to quasi-judicial decisions.

Advisory decisions are involved when a body has no formal decision-making power but is reviewing and commenting on a matter. Some advisory reviews are mandatory. For example, in North Carolina an initial zoning ordinance may not be adopted or sent to a public hearing by the governing board until it is recommended by a planning board.[4] Counties are required to send zoning ordinance amendments to a planning agency for a recommendation before adoption.[5] Other advisory reviews are optional. For example, special-use permit applications or subdivision plats may be sent to the planning board for comment before the city council acts on them. A draft administrative rule may be submitted to an advisory council before its consideration by a state commission. In all of these instances the advisory board takes a position that may significantly affect the

---

4. G.S. 160A-387, 153A-344.
5. G.S. 153A-344.

outcome of the land-use decision, but it does not actually make the decision, and there is no requirement that its recommendations be heeded.[6]

The second major category of land-use decision is legislative. The legislative decision involves policy choices that affect the entire community. The most typical is the adoption or the amendment of an ordinance by a local governing board[7] or an administrative rule by a state citizen commission. Courts traditionally have deferred to the governing board's judgment and to the political process with legislative decisions.[8]

The third type of decision by citizen boards is quasi-judicial. This type involves the application of adopted policies to individual situations. It must not entail new policy decisions, but apply previously made legislative decisions to the

---

6. In keeping with the requirements of the state's statute, a New Jersey court in Hochberg v. Borough of Freehold, 40 N.J. Super. 276, 123 A.2d 46 (1956), *cert. denied*, 22 N.J. 223, 125 A.2d 235, found that the fact that the planning board's action was advisory and the city council had to take final action did not remove the planning board from conflict-of-interest coverage. The Washington court reached a similar conclusion under its appearance-of-fairness doctrine [Buell v. City of Bremerton, 80 Wash. 2d 518, 495 P.2d 1358 (1972)]. However, other states have ruled that advisory decisions do not have to meet as strict procedural standards as other land-use decisions do. *See, e.g.*, Thompson v. Cook County Zoning Bd. of Appeals, 96 Ill. App. 3d 561, 421 N.E.2d 285 (1981). In such states advisory decisions may not be required to meet as strict a conflict-of-interest policy as legislative or quasi-judicial decisions must.

7. The courts have ruled that zoning is a governmental power that must be exercised by the elected board. In Harrington & Co. v. Ritter, 236 N.C. 321, 72 S.E.2d 838 (1952), the court held that a zoning ordinance could not be adopted by a special public-private group created by local legislation to zone the area around the Cherry Point military base, and in James v. Sutton, 229 N.C. 515, 50 S.E.2d 300 (1948), the court held that the power to zone could not be delegated by the governing board to the board of adjustment. Also, in *In re* Markham, 259 N.C. 566, 131 S.E.2d 329, *cert. denied*, 375 U.S. 931 (1964), the court ruled that a zoning ordinance amendment was a legislative matter within the discretion of the city council.

8. The court observed that in reviewing local ordinances, "[i]f fraud, dishonesty or oppression is charged against them, courts will be swift to investigate the charge, and to correct the evil, if found to exist. But other matters, involving mere questions of expediency and judgment, must be decided in another way" [State v. Austin, 114 N.C. 855, 860, 19 S.E. 919, 921 (1894) (upholding prohibition of minors in bars)]. The court noted that the other way was the electoral process. *See also* Jones v. Town of N. Wilkesboro, 150 N.C. 646, 64 S.E. 866 (1909) (allowing trial on challenge to water supply purchase); Clark's Greenville, Inc. v. West, 268 N.C. 527, 151 S.E.2d 5 (1966) (upholding Sunday-closing ordinance); Town of Atlantic Beach v. Young, 307 N.C. 422, 298 S.E.2d 686, *appeal dismissed*, 462 U.S. 1101 (1983) (upholding ban on horses and goats in city limits). Therefore resolution of bias and conflict-of-interest issues for legislative decisions is often guided more by legislatively adopted ethical guidelines than by strict legal rules set forth by the courts.

facts before the board.[9] Perhaps the most common example is a variance granted by a board of adjustment.[10] In North Carolina law the decision to issue or deny a special- or conditional-use permit, whether it is made by a board of adjustment[11] or an elected board,[12] also has been ruled to be quasi-judicial, as has approval of preliminary plats under local subdivision control ordinances.[13] Appeals of staff permit decisions to a board of adjustment or a state citizen commission also fall into this category.

For any quasi-judicial decision the courts require that all of the essential elements of a fair trial be observed, including developing a record of competent and substantial evidence to support the decision and giving parties directly affected by the decision the right to offer evidence, cross-examine witnesses, and have sworn testimony.[14] Because bodies exercising quasi-judicial functions do so with a degree of informality not present in the courts, the requirement for strict impartiality and fairness of the decision may be all the more important.[15]

Courts in several states have ruled that individual rezonings of relatively small areas are quasi-judicial decisions.[16] Given the site-specific nature of such decisions

---

9. In Lee v. Bd. of Adjustment, 226 N.C. 107, 37 S.E.2d 128 (1946), the court ruled that a board of adjustment could not approve a "nonconforming use" through a variance because that would be tantamount to amending the ordinance, which was a legislative decision reserved to the elected board.

10. *In re* Pine Hill Cemeteries, Inc., 219 N.C. 735, 15 S.E.2d 1 (1941).

11. Jackson v. Bd. of Adjustment, 275 N.C. 155, 166 S.E.2d 78 (1969); Keiger v. Bd. of Adjustment, 278 N.C. 17, 178 S.E.2d 616 (1971).

12. *In re* Application of Ellis, 277 N.C. 419, 178 S.E.2d 77 (1971).

13. Batch v. Town of Chapel Hill, 326 N.C. 1, 387 S.E.2d 655, *cert. denied*, 110 S. Ct. 2631 (1990). In practice most North Carolina local governments have treated subdivision plat approvals more as administrative than as quasi-judicial decisions.

14. Humble Oil & Refining Co. v. Bd. of Adjustment, 284 N.C. 458, 202 S.E.2d 129 (1974). Courts in other jurisdictions have explicitly held that quasi-judicial land-use decisions must observe a higher standard for disqualification due to conflicts of interest than legislative land-use decisions must. *See, e.g.*, Thornbury Twp. Bd. of Supervisors v. W.D.D., Inc., 119 Pa. Commw. 74, 546 A.2d 744 (1988).

15. NLRB v. Phelps, 136 F.2d 562 (5th Cir. 1943). The court noted:

> . . . [A] fair trial by an unbiased and nonpartisan trier of the facts is of the essence of the adjudicatory process as well when the judging is done in an administrative proceeding . . . as when it is done in a court by a judge. Indeed, if there is any difference, the rigidity of the requirement that the trier be impartial and unconcerned in the result applies more strictly to an administrative adjudication where many of the safeguards which have been thrown around court proceedings have, in the interest of expedition and supposed administrative efficiency been relaxed.
>
> [*Id.* at 563.]

16. *See, e.g.*, Fasano v. Bd. of County Comm'rs, 264 Or. 574, 507 P.2d 23 (1973).

and the findings that the governing board must make with small-area rezonings, North Carolina courts may eventually reach a similar conclusion. This is especially the situation with the creation of conditional-use zoning districts and spot zoning.[17]

In the context of creating conditional-use districts, the legislative/quasi-judicial distinction is further blurred by the common procedure of concurrently considering a rezoning to a conditional-use district (on its face a legislative decision) and a special-use permit for the proposed project in the new district (on its face a quasi-judicial decision). In fact, it is not altogether unusual in North Carolina local governments for a single motion to be made to approve both a rezoning and a special-use permit. In many ways such combined decisions are far more similar to quasi-judicial special-use permit decisions than to the broad legislative policy choices involved in typical ordinance adoptions. In this particular instance, then, the "legislative" designation may be more semantic than real, and the North Carolina courts may so rule in the future. In spot-zoning cases the North Carolina court has already moved away from strict deference to legislative decisions. In Chrismon v. Guilford County[18] the court ruled that differential zoning treatment for a relatively small area must be supported by a reasonable basis. Factors to be considered in determining the reasonableness of the rezoning decision include the size of the tract, the compatibility with the existing comprehensive zoning plan, the relation between the old and the new permitted uses, and the benefits and detriments of the new zoning for the landowner, the neighbors, and the community.[19] This case-by-case analysis by the courts of the underlying rationale for a legislative decision reflects the increasingly blurred boundaries between legislative and quasi-judicial land-use decisions.

---

17. *See* Chrismon v. Guilford County, 322 N.C. 611, 370 S.E.2d 579 (1988). On the contract-zoning aspects of the *Chrismon* case, see Comment, *Chrismon v. Guilford County and Hall v. City of Durham: Redefining Contract Zoning and Approving Conditional Use Zoning in North Carolina*, 68 N.C. L. REV. 177 (1989).

18. 322 N.C. 611, 370 S.E.2d 579 (1988).

19. *Id.* at 625–634.

CHAPTER THREE

Application of Conflict-of-Interest Law to Land-Use Management Decisions

Overview

Conflicts of interest in governmental decision making are hardly a new issue: in Plato's ideal government, ruling philosopher kings would have no outside financial entanglements.[1] In this country, although laws prohibiting citizens in government from taking official action for their private benefit date at least to an 1855 Massachusetts Senate rule forbidding members from voting on questions affecting their private rights,[2] most conflict-of-interest and general ethics laws have been adopted since 1950. Public and legislative attention to this issue has waxed and waned over the past forty years. The national pattern has been a highly publicized scandal (Sherman Adams in the 1950s, Bobby Baker in the 1960s, and Watergate in the 1970s being the most prominent examples), a flurry of legislative activity, and a lull until another scandal erupts ten or fifteen years later.[3]

---

1. PLATO, THE REPUBLIC 543C.
2. COUNCIL OF STATE GOVERNMENTS, ETHICS: STATE CONFLICT OF INTEREST/ FINANCIAL DISCLOSURE LEGISLATION 1972–75 1 (1975).
3. For a general historical review, see Baker, *The History of Congressional Ethics*, in REPRESENTATION AND RESPONSIBILITY: EXPLORING LEGISLATIVE ETHICS (B. Jennings and D. Callahan ed. 1985).

For reviews of the law in other states, see K. McVAY AND R. STUBBS, GOVERNMENTAL ETHICS AND CONFLICTS OF INTEREST IN GEORGIA (1980); Cooper, *The Alabama Ethics Act—Milestone or Millstone*, 5 CUMBERLAND-SAMFORD L. REV. 183 (1974); Kaufman and Widiss, *The California Conflict of Interest Laws*, 36 So. CAL. L. REV. 186 (1962); Nowlin, *Legislative Ethics, 1973*, 5 ST. MARY'S L.J. 456 (1973); Note, *State Legislative Conflicts of*

Land-use management decisions by local governments are especially vulnerable to conflicts of interest, given the large number of very substantial decisions that are made by volunteer citizen officials. Therefore it is not surprising that in several states considerable legislative and judicial attention has been given to the issue of conflict of interest in land-use decisions.[4] Unlike the intermittent, highly publicized national debates over ethics in government, attention by many state and local governments to the need to prevent the abuse of public trust in land-use decisions has been persistent over the past twenty years. Although the decisions of courts in a number of states are reviewed in this book, three states have the majority of the litigation on the subject: New Jersey, Connecticut, and Washington. New Jersey[5] and Connecticut[6] have since the early 1950s had relatively strict statutory requirements prohibiting conflicts of interest by planning

---

Interest: An Analysis of the Alabama Ethics Commission Recommendations, 23 ALA. L. REV. 369 (1971); Note, *Curbing Influence Peddling in Albany: The 1987 Ethics in Government Act*, 53 BROOKLYN L. REV. 1051 (1988); Note, *The Illinois Government Ethics Act—A Step Ahead Toward Better Government*, 22 DEPAUL L. REV. 302 (1972); Note, *State Conflict of Interest Laws: A Panacea for Better Government*, 16 DEPAUL L. REV. 453 (1967); Note, *Remedies for Conflicts of Interest among Public Officials in Iowa*, 22 DRAKE L. REV. 600 (1973); Note, *Conflicts of Interest of State Legislators*, 76 HARV. L. REV. 1209 (1963); Note, *Conflicts of Interest of State and Local Legislators*, 55 IOWA L. REV. 450 (1969); Comment, *Illinois Conflict of Interest Law and Municipal Officers*, 12 S. ILL. L.J. 571 (1988); Comment, *Texas Public Ethics Legislation: A Proposed Statute*, 50 TEX. L. REV. 931 (1972); Note, *Conflicts of Interest: A New Approach*, 18 U. FLA. L. REV. 675 (1966); Comment, *Legislative Conflicts of Interest—An Analysis of the Pennsylvania Legislative Ethics Code*, 19 VILLANOVA L. REV. 82 (1973); Note, *Conflict of Interest: State Government Employees*, 47 VA. L. REV. 1034 (1961).

4. R. ANDERSON, AMERICAN LAW OF ZONING §§ 4.19 to 4.21, 22.47 (3d ed. 1990); E. McQUILLAN, MUNICIPAL CORPORATIONS §§ 13.35, 25.57 (1986); 2 E. ZIEGLER, RATHKOPF'S THE LAW OF ZONING AND PLANNING, §§ 22.03, 22.04 (1989). For reviews of conflict-of-interest laws in other states as they relate to land-use decisions, see Gailey and Strom, *Conflicts of Interest on the Part of Zoning Decisionmakers*, 1983 ZONING AND PLANNING LAW HANDBOOK; and Tarlock, *Detecting and Challenging Bias in Zoning Board Decisions*, 1987 ZONING AND PLANNING LAW HANDBOOK.

For a collection of cases on several aspects of local government conflicts of interest generally, see Annotation, *Member of Government Board Voting on Measure Involving His Personal Interest*, 133 A.L.R. 1257 (1941); Annotation, *Disqualification for Bias or Interest of Administrative Officer Sitting in Zoning Proceedings*, 10 A.L.R.3d 694 (1966); and Annotation, *Disqualification of Judge by State, in Criminal Case, for Bias or Prejudice*, 68 A.L.R.3d 509 (1976).

5. New Jersey's statutory prohibition regarding conflicts of interest by planning boards provides, "No member of the planning board shall be permitted to act on any matter in which he has, either directly or indirectly, any personal or financial interest" [N.J. STAT. ANN. § 40:55D-23(b) (West)]. *See generally* Note, *Doctrine of Conflicting Interests Applied to Municipal Officials in New Jersey*, 12 RUTGERS L. REV. 582 (1958).

6. Connecticut's statute provides, "No member of any planning commission shall participate in the hearing or decision of the commission of which he is a member upon

boards, and consequently there has been considerable litigation interpreting those requirements. Since 1969 Washington has had a similarly strict, judicially established prohibition against conflicts of interest in land-use matters. Other states with conflict-of-interest statutes specifically addressing land-use decisions include Georgia, Idaho, Indiana, Kentucky, New Hampshire, New York, and Oregon.[7]

A majority of states require a citizen board member with a conflict of interest on a matter to be recused from that matter. *Recusation* is the legal term for a decision maker's being excused from hearing a matter because of conflict of interest, bias, or prejudice in the matter. It is broader than abstaining from voting, for it includes refraining from any participation in the debate on or the discussion of the matter. Some states allow limited participation if there is a disclosure of the conflict.

If a violation of conflict-of-interest standards is found, the typical remedy is for the court to invalidate the action taken by the citizen board and to remand the matter to the board for proper reconsideration.[8] Further a slight majority of the states addressing the question have ruled that participation in a land-use de-

---

any matter in which he is directly or indirectly interested in a personal or financial sense" [CONN. GEN. STAT. § 8-21]. A similar provision exists for zoning boards [CONN. GEN. STAT. § 8-11].

7.   GA. CODE ANN. §§ 36-67A-1 to -4; IDAHO CODE § 67-6506; IND. CODE §§ 36-7-4-223, 36-7-4-909; KY. REV. STAT. ANN. §§ 100.171, 100.221; N.H. REV. STAT. ANN. § 673:14; N.Y. GEN. MUN. LAW § 809 (McKinney); OR. REV. STAT. §§ 215.035, 227.035. Several additional states have adopted general conflict-of-interest or ethics codes. *See, e.g.,* CAL. GOV'T CODE § 87100 *et seq.*; COLO. REV. STAT. §§ 24-18-101 to -113; HAW. REV. STAT. § 84-14; MASS. ANN. LAWS ch. 268A, § 21A (Law. Coop.); VA. CODE ANN. § 2.1-639.14. Also, specific conflict-of-interest provisions for individual programs, such as urban renewal projects, are common. *See, e.g.,* IOWA CODE § 403.16; TEX. LOCAL GOV'T CODE ANN. § 374.908. A 1975 survey indicated that thirty-four states had adopted conflict-of-interest statutes between 1954 and 1975 [LEGISLATIVE RESEARCH COUNCIL OF MASSACHUSETTS, REPORT RELATIVE TO THE CONFLICT OF INTEREST LAW AND THE SEPARATION OF POWERS 28 (July 3, 1975)]. A 1983 survey reported forty-three states with conflict-of-interest statutes [S. HAYES, ETHICS PRACTICES IN SOUTH CAROLINA GOVERNMENT 6 (Public Affairs Bulletin No. 20, Bureau of Governmental Research and Service, University of South Carolina)]. For other surveys of state laws on conflicts of interest, see COUNCIL OF STATE GOVERNMENTS, ETHICS: STATE CONFLICT OF INTEREST/FINANCIAL DISCLOSURE LEGISLATION 1972–75 (1975); NATIONAL ASSOCIATION OF ATTORNEYS GENERAL, LEGISLATIVE APPROACHES TO CAMPAIGN FINANCE, OPEN MEETINGS AND CONFLICT OF INTEREST (December 1974); and NATIONAL ASSOCIATION OF ATTORNEYS GENERAL, LEGISLATION CONCERNING THE CORRUPTION OF PUBLIC OFFICIALS (Jan. 1974).

8.   *See, e.g.,* Smith v. City of Shelbyville, 462 N.E.2d 1052 (Ind. App. 1st Dist. 1984); Hallenborg v. Town Clerk of Billerica, 360 Mass. 513, 275 N.E.2d 525 (1971). The question of what remedies are available to a landowner whose project is delayed by a violation of the appearance-of-fairness doctrine was addressed by the Washington court in Alger v. City of Mukilteo, 107 Wash. 2d 541, 730 P.2d 1333 (1987). Although it voided the ordinance and allowed damages on other grounds, the court held that violation of the appearance-of-fairness doctrine did not give rise to a cause of action for

cision by a single member with an improper conflict of interest, even when the member's vote was not determinative, invalidates the action taken by the full board. The Washington court in Buell v. City of Bremerton[9] ruled that mere participation in the discussion by a planning board member with a financial conflict of interest tainted the proceedings and invalidated the rezoning, even though his vote had not been determinative of the outcome. Similarly a New Jersey court in Hochberg v. Borough of Freehold[10] found that an improper conflict of interest by one participating member of the planning board, even though that member's vote had not been required for the majority, infected all members and required invalidation of the rezoning. Also a New Jersey court ruled that invalidation was required when a council member with an improper conflict of interest secured introduction of a zoning amendment, even if the member subsequently abstained from voting on the final adoption of the amendment.[11]

This rule has been followed in New York,[12] Connecticut,[13] Iowa,[14] Wash-

---

damages against the governing board. A Georgia statute provides an interesting remedy for failure of a county governing board's members to disclose interests they have in property proposed for rezonings. If disclosure is not made within twenty days of the filing of a rezoning application, the member's office is declared vacant [1973 Ga. Laws, p. 3460, applicable to Cobb County]. This requirement was applied in Tendler v. Thompson, 256 Ga. 633, 352 S.E.2d 388 (1987).

Another potential remedy is a claim for monetary damages for violation of constitutionally protected rights to a fair hearing pursuant to 42 U.S.C.A. § 1983 (West 1981). In an employment termination case the North Carolina court upheld a dismissal, but awarded $78,000 in damages because of a biased discharge hearing [Crump v. Bd. of Education, 326 N.C. 603, 392 S.E.2d 579 (1990)].

For a review of alternative administrative enforcement mechanisms, see Rhodes, *Enforcement of Legislative Ethics: Conflict within the Conflict of Interest Laws*, 10 Harv. J. Legis. 373 (1973).

9.   80 Wash. 2d 518, 495 P.2d 1358 (1972).

10.   40 N.J. Super. 276, 123 A.2d 46 (1956), *cert. denied*, 22 N.J. 223, 125 A.2d 235.

11.   Netluch v. Mayor and Council of Borough of West Paterson, 130 N.J. Super. 104, 325 A.2d 517 (L. Div. 1974).

12.   Baker v. Marley, 8 N.Y.2d 365, 208 N.Y.S.2d 449, 170 N.E.2d 900 (1960). This case involved participation by a mayor in resolutions leading to the condemnation of property for a parking lot. The mayor owned less than a 1 percent interest in the property and offered to donate his share of the proceeds to the town. The court nonetheless held this to be an impermissible conflict.

13.   Bossert Corp. v. City of Norwalk, 157 Conn. 279, 253 A.2d 39 (1968); Daly v. Town Plan. and Zoning Comm'n, 150 Conn. 495, 191 A.2d 250 (1963); Low v. Town of Madison, 135 Conn. 1, 60 A.2d 774 (1948). *But see* Murach v. Plan. and Zoning Comm'n of City of New London, 196 Conn. 192, 491 A.2d 1058 (1985).

14.   Wilson v. Iowa City, 165 N.W.2d 813 (Iowa 1969). In this urban renewal case the court noted that the conflict-of-interest prohibition seeks to "demand complete

ington,[15] and New Hampshire.[16] Several other states, including Kentucky,[17] Pennsylvania,[18] Minnesota,[19] Kansas,[20] and Hawaii,[21] invalidate the action only if the improperly participating board member's vote was necessary for passage of the action. Because the public policy concern is promoting public confidence in the integrity of land-use decisions, the better course of action would seem to be invalidation of the action even if the member's vote was not necessary for passage. Once it is established that even a single member has improperly participated, the public perception is likely to be that the decision-making process has been tainted. The only way thereafter to restore the public confidence is to invalidate the action taken.

Apparent versus Actual Conflicts of Interest

One of the key questions in the conflict-of-interest area is whether an actual conflict of interest must be established to show a violation of the law or whether establishing a potential conflict or the appearance of a conflict is adequate. An actual conflict of interest is one that in fact motivates the member to vote for his

---

loyalty to the public interest and seek[s] to avoid subjecting a public servant to the difficult, and often insoluble, task of deciding between public duty and private advantage" [*Id.* at 822].

15.   Buell v. City of Bremerton, 80 Wash. 2d 518, 495 P.2d 1358 (1972).

16.   Winslow v. Holderness Planning Bd., 125 N.H. 262, 480 A.2d 114 (1984). In this case, which involved a subdivision approval, a member of the board had made public statements taking a position on the matter before a required quasi-judicial hearing. The court ruled that the member should have been disqualified and that his participation in the discussion had rendered the approval void, even though his vote had not been determinative. Some leeway may be given, however, in legislative decisions. In Michael v. City of Rochester, 119 N.H. 734, 407 A.2d 819 (1979), the court ruled that a legislative decision would be voided only if the vote of the member with a conflict was determinative of the outcome.

The North Carolina court applied the rule that one biased member's participation voids the entire board decision, in the context of a quasi-judicial personnel hearing [Crump v. Bd. of Education, 326 N.C. 603, 392 S.E.2d 579 (1990)].

17.   Sims v. Bradley, 309 Ky. 626, 218 S.W.2d 641 (1949) (mayor, whose wife owned property subject to rezoning petition and who was acting as her agent, could sit on zoning commission to establish quorum, and rezoning was valid so long as his vote was not required for adoption).

18.   Eways v. Reading Parking Auth., 385 Pa. 592, 124 A.2d 92 (1956) (ordinance was valid provided there were sufficient legal votes and no fraud or statutory restrictions were involved].

19.   Singewald v. Minneapolis Gas Co., 274 Minn. 556, 142 N.W.2d 739 (1966).

20.   Anderson v. City of Parsons, 209 Kan. 337, 496 P.2d 1333 (1972).

21.   Waikiki Resort Hotel v. City and County of Honolulu, 63 Haw. 222, 624 P.2d 1353 (1981).

or her personal interest rather than for the public benefit. An example is a governing board member's securing an option to purchase property and then maneuvering to have it rezoned to allow a more lucrative use solely for the purpose of being able to sell the property for a substantial profit. An apparent conflict of interest is a set of circumstances that would lead an independent observer to conclude that the member might have been motivated to act for self-interest, although whether he or she actually did or not is unknown. An example is a board member's participating in a decision on a proposal made by a third party to rezone an undeveloped parcel long owned by the member's family to a higher-intensity (and more lucrative) classification. An apparent conflict of interest also exists when a member votes on a matter without any consideration of the impact on his or her finances but the outcome nonetheless results in a substantial personal gain.

Courts are generally unwilling to inquire as to the motives of a particular action by a legislative body,[22] and proving that a conflict of interest actually motivated a decision is very difficult. So the decision to adopt a standard of review that prohibits the appearance of a conflict of interest has a significant bearing on the outcome of these cases.

The Supreme Court has ruled that avoidance of any appearance of conflict is required for the judiciary. In Tumey v. Ohio the court stated:

> . . . [T]he requirement of due process of law in judicial proceedings is not satisfied by the argument that men of the highest honor and the greatest self-sacrifice could carry it on without danger of injustice. Every procedure which would offer a possible temptation to the average man as a judge to forget the burden of proof . . . or which would lead him not to hold the balance nice, clear, and true . . . [denies due process of law].[23]

A majority of state courts that have addressed the issue have applied this principle to quasi-judicial land-use decisions.

The courts in Connecticut have ruled that citizen board members must refrain from putting themselves in positions in which personal interest may conflict with public duty. In Anderson v. Zoning Commission of Norwalk,[24] the court stated, "A public official owes an undivided duty to the public whom he serves,

---

22. *See, e.g.*, Wait v. Scottsdale, 127 Ariz. 107, 618 P.2d 601 (1980); Glen Cove Theatres, Inc. v. Glen Cove, 36 Misc. 2d 772, 233 N.Y.S.2d 972 (1962). It is often said, however, that there is an exception to this rule if there is any showing of fraud [Sheffield Development Co. v. Troy, 99 Mich. App. 527, 298 N.W.2d 23 (1980)]. *See generally* Annotation, *Motives: Inquiry, upon Review of Zoning Regulations, into Motive of Members of Municipal Authority Approving or Adopting It*, 71 A.L.R.2d 568 (1960); 2 J. DILLON, MUNICIPAL CORPORATIONS § 580 (5th ed. 1911). *See also* Comment, *Legislative Motive in Enacting Zoning Ordinance May Be Examined When Disclosed in Record of Public Hearing: The Exception Swallows the Rule*, 17 SYRACUSE L. REV. 687 (1966).

23. 273 U.S. 510, 532 (1926).

24. 157 Conn. 285, 253 A.2d 16 (1968).

and he is not permitted to place himself in a position which would subject him to conflicting duties or expose him to the temptation of acting in any manner other than in the best interest of the public."[25] The Connecticut court in Daly v. Town Plan Zoning Commission[26] further held that avoidance of even the appearance of impropriety is critical, noting that the state's policy on disqualification is concerned not only ". . . in influence improperly exercised but rather in the creation of a situation tending to weaken public confidence and to undermine the sense of security of individual rights which the property owner must feel assured will always exist in the exercise of zoning power."[27]

In the state of Washington the courts have developed a common law "doctrine of apparent fairness" to address bias and conflicts of interest in land-use decisions.[28] Application of this doctrine requires Washington citizen board members to avoid any hint of conflict of interest in quasi-judicial land-use decisions. In Washington, rezonings are considered quasi-judicial decisions, and there is a mandatory referral to the planning board before council action on them. In a series of cases the Washington Supreme Court has imposed strict standards on conflicts of interest to ensure completely impartial decisions on zoning amendments.

The Washington court noted that because zoning power so significantly affects landowners, strong steps should be taken to preserve public confidence in the way these decisions are made and to protect statutory guarantees for a "fair hearing" on these matters. Therefore the court ruled in Chrobuck v. Snohomish County[29] that not only actual conflicts of interest but any appearance of unfairness must be avoided, stating that it was concerned "not only in the elimination of actual bias, prejudice, improper influence or favoritism, but also in curbing the contradictions which, by their very existence, tend to create suspicion, generate misinterpretation and cast a pall of partiality, impropriety, conflict of interest or prejudgment. . . ."[30] In a subsequent case, Buell v. City of Bremerton,[31] the

---

25. *Id.* at 290, 253 A.2d at 19.

26. 150 Conn. 495, 191 A.2d 250 (1963).

27. *Id.* at 500, 191 A.2d at 252. In Mills v. Town Plan and Zoning Comm'n, 144 Conn. 493, 134 A.2d 250 (1957), the court ruled that conflicts must be avoided in all zoning-ordinance modifications, whether denominated legislative or quasi-judicial. Also, in Marmah, Inc. v. Town of Greenwich, 176 Conn. 116, 405 A.2d 63 (1978), the court held that if a governing board voting on a rezoning acted with predisposition and predetermination, the action was capricious, unreasonable, and illegal.

28. *See generally* Phillips, *The Appearance of Fairness Doctrine,* 20 URB. L. ANN. 75 (1980); Note, *Zoning Amendments and the Doctrine of Apparent Fairness,* 10 WILLAMETTE L. J. 348 (1974). *See also* American Cyanamid Co. v. FTC, 363 F.2d 757 (6th Cir. 1966).

29. 78 Wash. 2d 858, 480 P.2d 489 (1971).

30. *Id.* at 868, 480 P.2d at 495.

31. 80 Wash. 2d 518, 495 P.2d 1358 (1972).

court elaborated on this rationale, stating that planning commission members "must, as far as practicable, be open-minded, objective, impartial, free of entangling influences and capable of hearing the weak voices as well as the strong. . . . It is important not only that justice be done but that it also appear to be done."[32]

The test that the Washington court has adopted in applying this appearance-of-fairness doctrine in rezoning decisions, as stated in Swift v. Island County,[33] is, "Would a disinterested person, having been apprised of the totality of a board member's personal interest in a matter being acted upon, be reasonably justified in thinking that partiality may exist? If answered in the affirmative, such deliberations, and any course of conduct reached thereon, should be voided."[34]

The Washington court applies these very strict standards rigorously to quasi-judicial land-use decisions. The doctrine has also been applied to a degree in other contexts. In Smith v. Skagit County[35] the court distinguished between legislative and quasi-judicial decision making, noting that in the former the member's personal views and attitudes were acceptable and expected factors in their votes. But even with legislative decisions the court ruled that required hearings must be conducted with the "appearance of elemental fairness."[36] In this case the board met with proponents and excluded opponents after the required public hearing on a rezoning. The court ruled that this violated the requisite fairness and invalidated the rezoning. However, in Polygon Corp. v. City of Seattle,[37] it was held that the appearance-of-fairness doctrine did not apply to administrative decisions (such as issuance of a building permit) unless a public hearing was mandated. The court ruled that in administrative decisions there had to be a showing of actual partiality that precluded fair consideration of the application.

Other state courts have also emphasized the importance of avoiding even the appearance of impropriety when quasi-judicial land-use decisions are involved. For

---

32. *Id.* at 523, 495 P.2d at 1361.

33. 87 Wash. 2d 348, 552 P.2d 175 (1976).

34. *Id.* at 361, 552 P.2d at 183.

35. 75 Wash. 2d 715, 453 P.2d 832 (1969). *See also* City of Fairfield v. Superior Court, 14 Cal. 3d 768, 537 P.2d 375, 122 Cal. Rptr. 543 (1976); Wollen v. Borough of Fort Lee, 27 N.J. 408, 142 A.2d 881 (1958); Fiser v. City of Knoxville, 584 S.W.2d 659 (Tenn. App. 1979).

36. 75 Wash. 2d at 743, 453 P.2d at 848. *See also* Freeland v. Orange County, 273 N.C. 452, 160 S.E.2d 282 (1968), in which the court ruled that in a hearing on adoption of a zoning ordinance, it was permissible to limit the number of speakers and to impose a time limit on their remarks as long as the limits were fairly imposed on both proponents and opponents.

37. 90 Wash. 2d 59, 578 P.2d 1309 (1978). *See also* Zehring v. City of Bellevue, 103 Wash. 2d 588, 694 P.2d 638 (1985).

example, the Pennsylvania court ruled that appointment of a hearing board to review a conditional-use permit, which board was composed of a majority of members who had previously signed petitions opposing the project, created an impermissible appearance of unfairness.[38]

Courts in several other states have not taken such a strict position regarding governing boards avoiding apparent conflicts of interest when legislative land-use decisions are involved. In a case that presented the conflict-of-interest question for governing board members perhaps as clearly as any in the country, the Florida court in 1959 held that rezoning was a legislative decision and upheld a rezoning that substantially increased the value of one council member's property. In this case, Schauer v. City of Miami Beach,[39] the court upheld the rezoning even though the deciding vote was cast by a member whose property in the affected area was increased in value by $600,000 (in 1959 dollars) by the rezoning. The court ruled, "[O]nce the legislative nature of the action is established the barrier against judicial incursion is erected."[40] The dissent, however, concluded, "To give judicial approval to conduct so obviously opposed to the traditional standards of morals and ethics required of our public officials is to admit a failure in our judicial system," and it argued that the member had committed "a legal fraud against the people who trusted him."[41] The Virginia court in 1948 upheld a rezoning made at the request of a council member that allowed him to construct a gas station in an area previously zoned for exclusive residential use, noting that for such legislative decisions the council member should be answerable to the electorate, not the court.[42]

However, there are signs that judicial tolerance of conflicts of interest on legislative decisions may be waning. The Georgia court in 1974 held that label-

---

38. McVay v. Zoning Hearing Bd. of New Bethlehem Borough, 91 Pa. Commw. 287, 496 A.2d 1328 (1985). *See also* Thornbury Twp. Bd. of Supervisors v. W.D.D., Inc., 119 Pa. Commw. 74, 546 A.2d 744 (1988). An Indiana court ruled that circumstances that diminished public confidence in the zoning process could constitute an impermissible conflict of interest [Fail v. La Porte County Bd. of Zoning Appeals, 171 Ind. App. 192, 355 N.E.2d 455 (1976)].

39. 112 So. 2d 838 (Fla. 1959).

40. *Id.* at 839. For a note critical of this decision, see Note, *Municipal Corporations—Zoning—Disqualification of Councilman for Personal Interest*, 57 MICH. L. REV. 423 (1959). The author suggested that the court correctly held the rezoning to be a legislative decision, but contended that conflicts of interest should disqualify municipal governing board members from any zoning decision. For more recent legislative treatment of the matter in Florida, see Gonzalez and Claypool, *Voting Conflicts of Interest under Florida's Code of Ethics for Public Officers and Employees*, 15 STETSON L. REV. 675 (1986).

41. *Id.* at 842–843.

42. Blankenship v. Richmond, 188 Va. 97, 49 S.E.2d 321 (1948).

ing a zoning decision as "quasi-legislative," in this instance a rezoning decision, did not terminate an inquiry into disqualification due to financial interest and that a member with a direct or indirect interest in the outcome should be disqualified.[43] The court noted that only interests not shared by the public generally and not remote or speculative should trigger a disqualification in legislative land-use decisions.

Courts have generally restricted the prohibition against an appearance of conflict of interest to financial rather than ideological conflicts. For example, a New York court ruled that membership in a nonprofit corporation that was applying for a demolition permit did not disqualify a board member from participating in review of the application,[44] and an Oregon court found no conflict of interest for planning commission members who were formerly involved in a community planning organization that had recommended plan changes, or who had worked for a public agency interested in buying property later subject to a plan change.[45] However, in Save a Valuable Environment (SAVE) v. City of Bothell,[46] the Washington court addressed the question of membership in a group that had taken a position on an issue coming before the planning board. This case involved two planning board members who were active in the chamber of commerce, one as the staff executive director, the other as a member of the board of directors. Because the chamber of commerce had actively supported the rezoning involved, the court ruled that these members should not participate in planning board review of the application. A Pennsylvania court held that appointment of a board to review a conditional-use permit, a majority of whose members had previously signed petitions opposing the project, created an impermissible appearance of unfairness.[47]

---

43.   Olley Valley Estates, Inc. v. Fussell, 232 Ga. 779, 208 S.E.2d 801 (1974).

44.   Center Square Assoc., Inc. v. Corning, 105 Misc. 2d 6, 430 N.Y.S.2d 953 (1980). *But see* Tuxedo Conservation and Taxpayers Ass'n v. Town Bd. of the Town of Tuxedo, 69 A.D.2d 320, 418 N.Y.S.2d 638 (1979). The *Center Square* court emphasized the fact that a pecuniary interest rather than an appearance of impropriety should be controlling.

45.   Eastgate Theatre, Inc. v. Bd. of County Comm'rs, 37 Or. App. 745, 588 P.2d 640 (1978). The court held that the recusal standards for quasi-judicial decisions were not as strict as those for judicial decisions, noting both policy and statutory grounds for the distinction. *See also* Tierney v. Duris, 21 Or. App. 613, 536 P.2d 435 (1975).

46.   89 Wash. 2d 862, 576 P.2d 401 (1978).

47.   McVay v. Zoning Hearing Bd. of New Bethlehem Borough, 91 Pa. Commw. 287, 496 A.2d 1328 (1985).

Application to Various Types of Conflicts of Interest

Financial Conflicts of Interest

The extent or the size of financial interest required to create a conflict of interest is an issue that has proven difficult to quantify. In a 1926 case on conflicts of interest, Chief Justice William Howard Taft wrote that although self-interest should disqualify one from deciding a quasi-judicial matter, "[n]ice questions . . . arise as to what the degree or nature of the interest must be."[48] Justice Hugo Black added some thirty years later that although an interest in the outcome of a judicial proceeding disqualifies a judge, "[t]hat interest cannot be defined with precision. Circumstances and relationships must be considered."[49]

Direct conflicts such as voting on the rezoning of one's own property or the property of an employer are generally ruled impermissible for both legislative and quasi-judicial decisions. For example, in Kovalik v. Plan and Zoning Commission,[50] the chair of the zoning commission owned 697 acres (8 percent of the total area affected) being rezoned from one- to two-acre minimum lot sizes. The Connecticut court ruled that he was therefore disqualified. Similarly the Idaho court ruled that it was not proper for a planning board member to participate in a review of the siting of an electrical transmission line that would have crossed his property.[51]

---

48. Tumey v. Ohio, 273 U.S. 510, 522 (1926). The court has subsequently ruled that the financial interest need not be direct. In the *Tumey* case there was found to be an impermissible conflict when a mayor who served as a judge in traffic cases directly received fines. In Ward v. Village of Monroeville, 409 U.S. 57 (1972), the court ruled that an impermissible conflict also existed when the mayor served as judge and the fines collected formed a substantial part of the city's revenues.

49. *In re* Murchison, 349 U.S. 133, 136 (1955). As a commentator noted, "Much like 'sin,' few can define a conflict of interest, yet all are against it" [Comment, *Conflict of Interest*, 70 W. Va. L. Rev. 400, 400 (1968)].

50. 155 Conn. 497, 234 A.2d 838 (1965). *See also* Conrad v. Hinman, 122 Misc. 2d 531, 471 N.Y.S.2d 521 (1984), invalidating a variance under circumstances in which the board member was the co-owner of the property, and Piggott v. Hopewell, 22 N.J. Super. 106, 91 A.2d 667 (1952), holding that a variance granted by a town governing board was invalid because of the participation of a member who was the lessee of the property involved. *But see* Schauer v. City of Miami Beach, 112 So. 2d 838 (Fla. 1959); Blankenship v. Richmond, 188 Va. 97, 49 S.E.2d 321 (1948); Levitt & Sons v. Kane, 4 Pa. Commw. 375, 285 A.2d 917 (1972) (holding that elected official was not disqualified from voting on legislative rezoning simply because he owned property in affected zoning district).

51. Manookian v. Blaine County, 112 Idaho 697, 735 P.2d 1008 (1987). *See also* Zagores v. Conklin, 109 A.D.2d 281, 491 N.Y.S.2d 358 (2d Dep't 1985), in which it

A majority of state courts have held that modest or insignificant financial interests do not disqualify a member from participating in land-use decisions, particularly legislative ones. For example, all residents of a city are to some degree financially affected by the initial adoption of a zoning ordinance. If such general and modest impacts disqualified a person from participating in the ordinance's adoption, no one could vote on it.[52]

The New Jersey decisions on this question illustrate the difficulty in defining the size of financial interest required to constitute impermissible conflict of interest. In two 1956 cases involving legislative land-use decisions, the court found an impermissible conflict. Hochberg v. Borough of Freehold[53] involved a planning board's mandatory review of a rezoning that would have allowed expansion of a racetrack. One member of the planning board operated a concession stand for workers at the track. The court judged that his participation in review of the proposed rezoning violated the state's nonparticipation statute, ruling that a financial interest in the outcome, even if small and indirect, required disqualification of the member. Aldom v. Borough of Roseland[54] applied the same standard to a governing board on a common-law rather than a statutory basis. In this case the governing board member had a conflict of interest based upon being an employee of the owner of a tract being rezoned.

Decisions two years later, however, emphasized that minor financial interests do not always trigger the New Jersey nonparticipation statute. In Wilson v. Long Branch[55] the court ruled that planning board members who were officers and shareholders in banks holding mortgages in areas affected by a recommendation to establish a redevelopment area, and board members who were nearby residents, might vote because their financial interest in the outcome was so re-

---

was ruled that employees of a utility company seeking approval to convert generating units from oil to coal burning should not participate in the board of appeals consideration of a variance for the project, and Baker v. Marley, 8 N.Y.2d 365, 208 N.Y.S.2d 449, 170 N.E.2d 900 (1960). In Sokolinski v. Municipal Council of Woodbridge, 192 N.J. Super. 101, 469 A.2d 96 (1983), it was held to be improper for board members who were either employees of the school board or spouses of employees of the school board to participate in the consideration of a variance for school property that was being sold.

52. *But see* Thorne v. Zoning Comm'n of Town of Old Saybrook, 178 Conn. 198, 423 A.2d 861 (1979). The zoning change challenged in this case was part of a comprehensive revision of the entire town's zoning. The court ruled that there was no exception to the rule of nonparticipation in any matter in which a board member had an interest. The rule applies to comprehensive ordinance revisions as well as to the rezoning of individual sites.

53. 40 N.J. Super. 276, 123 A.2d 46 (1956), *cert. denied*, 22 N.J. 223, 125 A.2d 235.

54. 42 N.J. Super. 495, 127 A.2d 190 (App. Div. 1956).

55. 27 N.J. 360, 142 A.2d 837, *cert. denied*, 385 U.S. 873 (1958).

mote and contingent as not to constitute a conflict. In Van Itallie v. Borough of Franklin Lakes,[56] the court held that a governing board member was not disqualified because he owned property adjacent to an applicant's property, in the absence of a showing of impact on the member.

Subsequent New Jersey cases have continued the attempt to draw a line between substantial and insignificant financial interests. In Toutphoeus v. Joy[57] the court ruled that service as real estate broker on a property a year before a rezoning application was filed did not automatically trigger the nonparticipation statute. In Dover Township Homeowners and Tenants Association v. Dover Township,[58] a planning board action was invalidated because of the participation of a member who was the manager of a title insurance company that had done all of the title work for the applicant.

Courts in other states have also struggled with these essentially ad hoc determinations of how large a financial interest is necessary to trigger a conflict of interest. The Washington court in Buell v. City of Bremerton[59] overturned a rezoning in which a planning board member's nearby property would have increased in value if the proposed commercial rezoning had been adopted. However, in Narrowsview Preservation Association v. City of Tacoma,[60] the court ruled that a council member who was a former employee of the applicant could participate in the decision because mere acquaintance or casual business dealings in a minimal sense were not in and of themselves a disqualifying conflict of interest. The Connecticut court ruled in Dana-Robin Corp. v. Common Council, City of Danbury[61] that a board member was not disqualified from voting on a rezoning for a multifamily housing project on the basis of his ownership of another multifamily housing project. The court found that the proposed project, because of its location and likely market, was not competitive with the board member's preexisting project. A similar finding was made in regard to a second board member who also owned rental property.

---

56. 28 N.J. 258, 146 A.2d 111 (1958).

57. 81 N.J. Super. 526, 196 A.2d 250 (1963). In this case the chairman of the board had served as the realtor when the applicant had bought the property the previous year, but he had no continuing interest in the property. He voluntarily abstained from voting, but did not leave the room and did sign the resolution in his official capacity as chairman. The court upheld the board's decision.

58. 114 N.J. Super. 270, 276 A.2d 156 (App. Div. 1971).

59. 80 Wash. 2d 518, 495 P.2d 1358 (1972).

60. 84 Wash. 2d 416, 526 P.2d 897 (1974), rev'd on other grounds, Norway Hill Preservation and Protection Ass'n v. King County Council, 87 Wash. 2d 267, 552 P.2d 674 (1976).

61. 166 Conn. 207, 348 A.2d 560 (1974).

Courts addressing this issue in other states, including Colorado,[62] Nebraska,[63] Massachusetts,[64] and New Hampshire,[65] have ruled that only interests that substantially influence a decision should be considered impermissible conflicts. The Oklahoma court ruled that a planning commissioner should not have been disqualified from voting on a rezoning for a customer of his, even though a denial of the rezoning would have adversely affected his business.[66] Similarly a California court held that there was no improper conflict of interest when one member of a planning commission recommending a rezoning owned a bar in the area being rezoned and another member was an officer in a title insurance company that held legal title to property in the area.[67] In Iowa the court interpreted related statutes to exempt board of adjustment members from conflict-of-interest coverage for quasi-judicial decisions if they owned less than a five percent interest in a company appearing before the board.[68] In Pennsylvania a court ruled that an interest must be immediate and direct to warrant disqualification from a legislative decision, judging that ownership of a home on a six-acre tract that was included in a 500-acre rezoning did not require recusal, absent a showing of any particular pecuniary benefit to the council member.[69]

---

62.   Best v. LaPlata Plan. Comm'n, 701 P.2d 91 (Colo. App. 1984). The court ruled that there was a presumption of integrity, honesty, and impartiality in favor of those serving in quasi-judicial capacities. No conflict was found in a situation in which a board member had been a member of the law firm that represented the developer before her election to the board, but had not at any time actually represented the developer and was no longer a member of the law firm. *See also* Strandberg v. Kansas City, 415 S.W.2d 737 (Mo. 1967), for a similar ruling allowing the mayor's participation in a rezoning petition under circumstances in which his law partner had represented the applicant in the matter before the mayor's election.

63.   Copple v. City of Lincoln, 202 Neb. 152, 274 N.W.2d 520 (1979).

64.   Mass. Gen. L. ch. 268A, § 21(a), applied in Crall v. City of Leominster, 362 Mass. 95, 284 N.E.2d 610 (1972). *See also* Buss, *The Massachusetts Conflict of Interest Statute: An Analysis*, 45 B.U. L. Rev. 299 (1965).

65.   Sherman v. Town of Brentwood, 112 N.H. 122, 290 A.2d 47 (1972). In this case the New Hampshire court ruled that a member of a board of adjustment who worked for a county surplus food program could participate in hearing a variance request for an addition to the county hospital because there was no showing that his job was in any way related to the application.

66.   Hoffman v. Stillwater, 461 P.2d 944 (Okla. 1969).

67.   Orinda Homeowners Comm. v. Bd. of Supervisors, 11 Cal. App. 3d 768, 90 Cal. Rptr. 88 (1970). In this case there was no showing that either planning board member had any financial interest in the outcome of the advisory decision on the rezoning.

68.   Helmke v. Bd. of Adjustment, 418 N.W.2d 346 (Iowa 1988).

69.   Levitt & Sons v. Kane, 4 Pa. Commw. 375, 285 A.2d 917 (1972).

In Wyman v. Popham,[70] however, a Georgia court held that a charge that two of three members of a county board of commissioners voting for a rezoning had sold the applicant goods and services was a sufficient allegation of fraud and corruption to warrant a trial on the issue. The court ruled that given the importance of zoning to both the public and property owners, the general rule of not inquiring into the motives of members making legislative decisions should not be followed. Further the court ruled that given the subtle nature of fraud in land-use decisions, those challenging the action needed to do so only by a preponderance of the evidence.

One approach to the uncertainty as to when a financial interest is sufficient to warrant disqualification is to define the issue statutorily. The California Political Reform Act prohibits state and local government officials from participating or attempting to influence any decision in which they have a financial interest. Such an interest is deemed to exist when it is reasonably foreseeable that the decision will have a material effect, distinguishable from its effect on the public generally, on the member or the member's immediate family. Such an effect is automatically presumed if the decision will directly affect a business or property interest valued at more than $1,000, an income source of $250 or more per year, or any business that the member owns or manages or by which the member is employed.[71]

Business Ties to Applicants

A form of conflict of interest that is closely related to the direct financial conflicts just discussed is the indirect financial benefit resulting from close business ties to an applicant that may or may not eventually directly benefit a member. Even though a citizen board member may not directly benefit financially, most courts equate current or past close business ties to an applicant to a financial interest in the land-use decision that can disqualify a member from participation. For example, the New Jersey court ruled in Bracy v. Long Branch[72] that a board member who was the architect for a housing authority should not vote on matters affecting the authority.

The Connecticut court established this principle in a series of cases in the 1960s. In Josephson v. Planning Board of Stanford,[73] the court ruled that a

---

70. 252 Ga. 247, 312 S.E.2d 795 (1984). *See also* Olley Valley Estates v. Fussell, 232 Ga. 779, 208 S.E.2d 801 (1974), in which the court ruled that to be impermissible, the interest must not be one shared by the public generally and must not be remote or speculative.

71. CAL. GOV'T CODE § 87103 (West 1987).

72. 73 N.J. Super. 91, 179 A.2d 63 (1962).

73. 151 Conn. 489, 199 A.2d 690, 10 A.L.R. 3d 687 (1964).

planning board member had to be disqualified from voting on a rezoning/plan amendment because the landowner was represented by a realtor who shared an office with the board member. In 1967 in Kloter v. Zoning Commission[74] it was held that prior representation of an applicant as an accountant and close advisor in real estate matters disqualified a board member from participation in consideration of a rezoning; and in 1968 in Bossert Corp. v. Norwalk[75] it was held that a city council member had to be disqualified because his law partner represented the opponents to a rezoning. In this later case the court ruled that mere abstention was not sufficient, that either the law firm had to withdraw from representing the party or the council member had to resign. The court tempered the rule somewhat in Anderson v. Zoning Commission of Norwalk[76] in 1968, finding no conflict of interest when a planning board member's company employed an attorney who was also employed by an applicant. The court noted:

> Local governments would . . . be seriously handicapped if any conceivable interest, no matter how remote and speculative, would require the disqualification of a zoning official. If this were so it would not only discourage but might prevent capable men and women from serving as members of the various zoning authorities. Of course, courts should scrutinize the circumstances with great care and should condemn anything which indicates the likelihood of corruption or favoritism. They must, however, also be mindful that to abrogate a municipal action on the basis that some remote and nebulous interest may be present would be to deprive unjustifiably a municipality, in many important instances, of the services of its duly-elected or appointed officials.[77]

The Washington courts have a similar line of cases from the 1970s applying a very strict standard prohibiting business relations that present even the appearance of unfairness in quasi-judicial decisions. In Fleming v. City of Tacoma,[78] the court found an improper conflict of interest when a city council member was hired as an attorney for a rezoning proponent forty-eight hours after the rezoning decision, even though there was no evidence of any prior contacts. In Narrowsview Preservation Association v. City of Tacoma,[79] the court held that it was impermissible for a city council member to participate in a rezoning decision when he was

---

74.   26 Conn. Supp. 495, 227 A.2d 563 (1967).

75.   157 Conn. 279, 253 A.2d 39 (1968). *But see* Kiss v. Bd. of Appeals, 371 Mass. 147, 355 N.E.2d 461 (1976), in which the court held that there was no conflict of interest when the zoning board chairman's law firm represented the estate of one of the sellers of property subject to a zoning permit but the chairman only presided at the hearing and did not vote on the matter.

76.   157 Conn. 285, 253 A.2d 16 (1968).

77.   *Id.* at 291, 253 A.2d at 20.

78.   81 Wash. 2d 292, 502 P.2d 327 (1972).

79.   84 Wash. 2d 416, 526 P.2d 897 (1974), *rev'd on other grounds*, Norway Hill

employed by a bank that held the mortgage on a property whose value would be doubled by the rezoning. Similarly in Swift v. Island County[80] an impermissible conflict was found when a governing board member had substantial financial interests in the mortgagee of the proposed project. In Hayden v. City of Port Townsend[81] an impermissible conflict was found when a planning board member was the manager of a bank seeking to expand. The bank held an option on property that had to be rezoned to allow the expansion. In this case the member with the conflict participated in an initial favorable recommendation of the rezoning to the governing board. After a conflict-of-interest question was raised, the governing board rescinded its approval and remanded the ordinance to the planning board for reconsideration. On reconsideration the member with the conflict stepped down, but spoke as a "private citizen" in favor of the rezoning before both the planning board and the governing board. The court ruled that the appearance-of-fairness doctrine was still violated because it required not only abstention from voting but total nonparticipation in the hearing and decision-making process.[82]

A New York case, Tuxedo Conservation and Taxpayers Association v. Town Board of the Town of Tuxedo,[83] also addressed this question of existing and potential business dealings with an applicant as grounds for finding an improper conflict of interest. In this case the court ruled that a governing board member who was employed by an advertising company that had the applicant's parent corporation for a client should not participate in matters involving the applicant's project. The court found that even though the board member himself did not directly work on any projects for that client and even though future advertising contracts for his company should the project be constructed were speculative,

---

Preservation and Protection Ass'n v. King County Council, 87 Wash. 2d 267, 552 P.2d 674 (1976). The court ruled that a violation was established by showing an interest that "might have substantially influenced a member of the commission even if that interest did not actually affect him" [*Id.* at 420, 526 P.2d at 901]. In this case the court also ruled that a second council member who was a former employee of the applicant could participate in the decision.

80.   87 Wash. 2d 348, 552 P.2d 175 (1976).

81.   28 Wash. App. 192, 622 P.2d 1291 (1981).

82.   The New Jersey court also invalidated an action in which a member abstained from voting but participated in the discussion [Netluch v. Mayor and Council of Borough of West Paterson, 130 N.J. Super. 104, 325 A.2d 517 (Law Div. 1974)]. However, the Rhode Island and Wisconsin courts have upheld actions in which a member with a conflict testified or participated in the discussion but did not vote [Tramonti v. Zoning Bd. of Review, 93 R.I. 131, 172 A.2d 93 (1961); Ballenger v. Door County, 131 Wis. 2d 422, 388 N.W.2d 624 (1986)].

83.   69 A.D.2d 320, 418 N.Y.S.2d 638 (1979). For a discussion of the planning issues involved, told from the perspective of the attorneys for the developer of the proposed project, see R. BABCOCK AND C. SIEMON, THE ZONING GAME REVISITED 11–35 (1985).

participation created an appearance of impropriety. The court noted, "Was [his] vote prompted by the 'jingling of the guinea' or did he vote his conscience as a member of the Town Board? In view of the factual circumstances involved, the latter possibility strains credulity. For, like Caesar's wife, a public official must be above suspicion."[84]

Nonfinancial Relationships with Applicants

Financial considerations and business ties are not the only factors that may create a conflict of interest for citizen board members. A close nonfinancial relationship with the parties involved in a land-use decision may also create impermissible bias.

A 1956 New Jersey decision clearly set forth this rule. In Zell v. Borough of Roseland,[85] the court held that a planning board member should be disqualified from voting on a rezoning of property owned by a church at which he was a parishioner. The court stated that the concern with potential conflict of interest was not confined to matters of possible financial gain but included any matter that might exert an undue influence on the decision.

Close family ties have also long been held to create impermissible conflicts of interest. In 1948 in Low v. Town of Madison,[86] the Connecticut court ruled that a board member should not participate in a decision on a rezoning applied for by his spouse. In Thorne v. Zoning Commission of Town of Old Saybrook,[87] the court ruled that it was improper for a member to participate in consideration of a rezoning when the property was in close proximity to his parents' and sister's

---

84.   418 N.Y.S.2d at 640.

85.   42 N.J. Super. 75, 125 A.2d 890 (1956). *See also* McVoy v. Bd. of Adjustment, 213 N.J. Super. 109, 516 A.2d 634 (1986), for a more recent similar ruling. Not all relationships create improper conflicts of interest. For example, see Armstrong v. Zoning Bd. of Appeals, 158 Conn. 158, 257 A.2d 799 (1969) [neither service as chair of nonprofit group that was urging funding for mental health programs nor having child that had previously been patient of applicant foundation at another site disqualified members from considering permit from applicant to operate school]; McGavin v. Zoning Bd. of Appeals, 26 Conn. Supp. 251, 217 A.2d 229 (1965) [friendship with opponent to variance did not in itself disqualify board member].

86.   135 Conn. 1, 60 A.2d 774 (1948). This case involved a rezoning from residential to business use. The court concluded:

> The good faith of the official is of no moment because it is the policy of the law to keep him so far from the temptation as to insure the exercise of unselfish public interest. He must not be permitted to place himself in a position in which personal interest may conflict with his public duty.
> [*Id.* at 8, 60 A.2d at 777.]

87.   178 Conn. 198, 423 A.2d 861 (1979).

residences and he had expressed an interest in maintaining the character of their neighborhood. A Washington court addressed family associations in Fleck v. King County,[88] holding that persons married to each other should not serve on the same board of appeals because their votes might appear to be based in part on their relationship and not on the facts of the individual case before the board. A New Jersey court ruled that a council member should not participate in a rezoning decision involving a nursing home in which his mother resided.[89] Similar restrictions based on family relations have been established by the New York court.[90] A California court held that it was permissible for the city council to remove a planning commissioner from office upon the election of her husband to the city council in order to prevent the appearance of a conflict of interest.[91]

Courts have invalidated quasi-judicial land-use decisions tainted by the appearance of a "higher" political figure in the matter. In Place v. Board of Adjustment,[92] the New Jersey court ruled it was improper for the mayor who had appointed a board of adjustment to appear before the board as the attorney for a client objecting to the issuance of a variance. A Michigan court reached a similar conclusion regarding the appearance of a governing board member before a

---

88. 16 Wash. App. 668, 558 P.2d 254 (1977).

89. Barrett v. Union Twp. Comm., 230 N.J. Super. 195, 553 A.2d 62 (1989). See also Kremer v. City of Plainfield, 101 N.J. Super. 346, 244 A.2d 335 (1968) (nephew of planning board member was partner in law firm representing applicant). However, in Van Itallie v. Borough of Franklin Lakes, 28 N.J. 258, 146 A.2d 111 (1958), a member was not disqualified on the basis that his brother was a lower-level employee of the accountant firm for the applicant. In Schweihofer v. Zachary, 103 Mich. App. 792, 303 N.W.2d 896 (1981), the Michigan court found such a relationship (in this case an uncle of someone appearing before the board of appeals) not to be an automatic disqualifier. See also Carr v. City of Eldorado, 217 Ark. 423, 230 S.W.2d 485 (1950) (mayor's son serving as attorney for taxicab-permit applicant did not automatically disqualify mayor). If the family member on the board recuses himself or herself, there is no conflict of interest for the remainder of the board [Application of Richards, 41 Misc. 2d 850, 246 N.Y.S.2d 746 (1962)].

90. Engleston S. Van Lieve, Inc. v. Village of Sodus Point, 135 A.D.2d 1141, 523 N.Y.S.2d 269 (4th Dep't 1987) (board member's son was married to daughter of witness).

91. Kimura v. Roberts, 89 Cal. App. 3d 871, 152 Cal. Rptr. 569 (1979).

92. 42 N.J. 324, 200 A.2d 601 (1964). The case involved a variance from a side-yard setback requirement for a fallout shelter. A New Hampshire ethics opinion similarly ruled that a lawyer member of a governing board could not appear before that local government's planning board or board of adjustment on behalf of a client. The opinion went on to rule that the board member's law partners could appear before such an appointed board but only if the governing board member publicly disqualified himself or herself from the matter and refrained from participating in any related governing board matters, including appointment of members of the planning board and the board of adjustment [Ethics Comm., New Hampshire Bar Ass'n, Op. 1988-9/12 (Feb. 9, 1989)].

zoning board appointed by the council.[93] A federal district court overturned a board of adjustment decision by the District of Columbia to grant approval for the construction of an embassy in a residential zone under circumstances in which several board members (who were subordinate government employees) were contacted outside the hearing process and advised that high government officials favored the project.[94] The court noted that the board members

> were made to know that a favorable decision would be pleasing, and an unfavorable decision displeasing, to persons in very high government brackets . . . . The pressures were not crudely or indelicately exerted. There was no threat or command. There was no promise of reward. But the pressures were nevertheless real . . . . Contacts of this kind, regrettably, are not new. Some are the products of venality and corruption. Those involved herein were not . . . . However, the end result is the same . . . .[95]

The court described the practice of assuring the people contacted that there was no intent to ask them to do other than their duty, and then expressing a hope that their duty would incline them in the desired direction, as a "soft touch," and ruled that it deprived the parties of a fair and impartial hearing. These cases involving alleged exertion of improper political influence by a superior official must be distinguished from allegations that the land-use action was taken in response to the political pressures of citizens. In the latter instance the courts have generally ruled that the action is valid.[96]

An interesting question is presented by ethical codes that have the effect of restricting associational rights of citizen board members to ensure fairness in land-use decisions. A New York court has held that a town board has the authority to adopt an ethics code prohibiting officers in political parties from serving on a zoning board of adjustment.[97]

---

93. Barkey v. Nick, 11 Mich. App. 381, 161 N.W.2d 445 (1968). *See also* Abrahamson v. Wendell, 72 Mich. App. 80, 249 N.W.2d 302 (1976), *on rehearing,* 76 Mich. App. 278, 256 N.W.2d 613 (1977) [appearance of township supervisor before zoning board of appeals as contractor for applicant constituted improper duress on board].

94. Jarrott v. Scrivener, 225 F. Supp. 827 (D.D.C. 1964).

95. *Id.* at 834.

96. *See, e.g.,* Burns v. Des Peres, 534 F.2d 103 (8th Cir. 1976), *cert. denied,* 429 U.S. 861; Warren v. Marietta, 249 Ga. 205, 288 S.E.2d 562 (1982); Mettee v. County Comm'rs of Howard County, 212 Md. 357, 129 A.2d 136 (1957); Montgomery County v. Horman, 46 Md. App. 491, 418 A.2d 1249 (1980). Also a Pennsylvania court ruled that being a candidate for the governing board did not disqualify a member of the zoning board [Danwell Corp. v. Zoning Hearing Bd., 115 Pa. Commw. 174, 540 A.2d 588, *appeal denied,* 520 Pa. 620, 554 A.2d 511 (1988)].

97. Belle v. Town Bd. of Onondaga, 61 A.D.2d 352, 402 N.Y.S.2d 677 (1978). *See generally* Broadrick v. Oklahoma, 413 U.S. 601 (1973), regarding states' authority

Also, campaign contributions, as opposed to contacts by political figures on an individual case, have generally been held not to be a conflict of interest for elected officials who must subsequently make quasi-judicial land-use decisions. This policy has been followed in New Jersey,[98] Washington,[99] California,[100] and Hawaii.[101]

Prior Opinions, Ex Parte Communications, and the Hearing Process

To ensure fair and impartial land-use decisions, courts have also examined the impact of prejudgment by citizen board members and the conduct of the hearing process. Several courts have invalidated quasi-judicial land-use decisions when a board member expressed an opinion before the required hearing. In Lake Garda Improvement Association v. Town Plan and Zoning Commission,[102] the Connecticut court ruled that a board member who had sued an association that was challenging a rezoning and who had continued to express an antagonistic attitude toward the group should have been disqualified from participation in the rezoning. The Rhode Island court invalidated a variance granted under circumstances in which a board member had told a neighbor who opposed a project before a formal application had been filed that the project was going to be approved.[103] The New Hampshire court invalidated a subdivision approval

---

to restrict the partisan political activities of their officers and employees, and Buckley v. Valeo, 424 U.S. 1 (1976), regarding limitations on authority to regulate political contributions.

98.   Wollen v. Borough of Fort Lee, 27 N.J. 408, 142 A.2d 881 (1958).

99.   Westside Hilltop Survival Comm. v. King County, 96 Wash. 2d 171, 634 P.2d 862 (1981).

100.   Woodland Hills Residents Ass'n v. City Council of the City of Los Angeles, 26 Cal. 3d 938, 609 P.2d 1029 (1980). The case is reviewed in Note, *Woodland Hills v. City Council of Los Angeles: Electoral Politics and Quasi-Judicial Fairness*, 69 CAL. L. REV. 1098 (1981); Comment, *The Appearance of Fairness Doctrine: Closing a Loophole in California's Political Reform Act*, 17 CAL. W.L. REV. 75 (1980).

101.   Life of the Land, Inc. v. City Council of the City and County of Honolulu, 61 Haw. 390, 606 P.2d 866 (1980).

102.   151 Conn. 476, 199 A.2d 162 (1964). The court also noted that the board member's personal friendship and business dealings with the applicant were further grounds for recusal. *See also* Lage v. Zoning Bd. of Appeals, 148 Conn. 597, 172 A.2d 911 (1961). *But see* Holt-Lock, Inc. v. Zoning and Plan. Comm'n, 161 Conn. 182, 286 A.2d 299 (1971), in which the court ruled that service on a separate town commission that had previously discussed the matter and had made a recommendation on it to the zoning commission did not disqualify a member who sat on both commissions.

103.   Barbara Realty Co. v. Zoning Bd. of Review of Cranston, 85 R.I. 152, 128 A.2d 342 (1957). The court held that the power to grant variances was a "delicate duty"

based on a board member's having taken a position on the project before the required quasi-judicial hearing.[104] In Furtney v. Simsbury Zoning Commission,[105] however, the Connecticut court ruled that an opinion expressed as to the suitability of a site three years before a rezoning request was not automatically an impermissible bias. The court concluded that the law did not require the board member to have no opinion on the proper development of the community. The test rather was whether the member had a firm and fixed opinion that would not be affected by the hearing.

For legislative decisions, prior expression of opinions has generally been held not to constitute impermissible bias.[106] On the contrary, free and candid expression of views by candidates in the electoral process is encouraged. A Texas court ruled that preelection campaign promises opposing construction of more apartments did not disqualify members elected to office from participation in subsequent consideration of rezoning property from apartment to low-density residential.[107] These decisions allowing the member's participation generally have not involved any element of personal gain, however. If that factor is present, a different result may obtain. A New Jersey court ruled that a governing board member had to be disqualified from voting on a rezoning, given that he had actively opposed the proposed use before joining the council *and* he owned property in the immediate vicinity of the site.[108]

---

that "must be exercised with strict impartiality or there will inevitably result a loss of public confidence in the policy of the zoning ordinance and in the integrity of the officials charged with the responsibility of administering it" [*Id.* at 156, 128 A.2d at 344].

104. Winslow v. Holderness Plan. Bd., 125 N.H. 262, 480 A.2d 114 (1984).

105. 159 Conn. 585, 271 A.2d 319 (1970). *See also* General Cinema Corp. v. Foley, 60 A.D.2d 856, 401 N.Y.S.2d 249 (1978), in which it was held that the chairman of a zoning board of appeals expressing general antipathy toward related signs early in a hearing on an application for a variance for a sign did not constitute impermissible bias.

106. City of Fairfield v. Superior Ct., 14 Cal. 3d 768, 537 P.2d 375, 122 Cal. Rptr. 5543 (1976); Binford v. Western Electric Co., 219 Ga. 404, 133 S.E.2d 361 (1964); Turf Valley Assoc. v. Zoning Bd., 262 Md. 632, 278 A.2d 574 (1971); Moskow v. Boston Redevelopment Auth., 349 Mass. 553, 210 N.E.2d 699 (1965); Wollen v. Borough of Fort Lee, 27 N.J. 408, 142 A.2d 881 (1958); Fiser v. City of Knoxville, 584 S.W.2d 659 (Tenn. App. 1979). *See also* Ass'n of Nat'l Advertisers v. FTC, 627 F.2d 1151 (D.C. Cir. 1979), *cert. denied*, 447 U.S. 921 (1980) [prior strong opinion did not disqualify commissioners from rule making on children's advertising on television]. For a detailed discussion of the difficulties inherent in applying bias and conflict-of-interest standards to legislative decisions, see Strauss, *Disqualification of Decisional Officials in Rulemaking*, 80 COLUM. L. REV. 990 (1980).

107. City of Farmer's Branch v. Hawnco, Inc., 435 S.W.2d 288 (Tex. Civ. App. 1968).

108. McNamara v. Saddle River, 60 N.J. Super. 367, 158 A.2d 722, *aff'd*, 64 N.J. Super. 426, 166 A.2d 391 (1960).

Improprieties in the process of making land-use decisions have also been held to create impermissible conflicts of interest. Prior contacts and improper lobbying were addressed in the Washington case of Chrobuck v. Snohomish County.[109] The court ruled that an improper conflict of interest existed when planning board members were entertained by a rezoning proponent and then announced their support for the rezoning before the public hearing. The Washington courts have also emphasized the importance of ensuring a fair procedure for the consideration of these quasi-judicial rezonings. For example, a rezoning was invalidated in Anderson v. Island County[110] because the governing board at the public hearing interrupted opponents of the rezoning, advised the opponents of the board's intent to approve the rezoning, and cut off the hearing before all the opposing testimony had been received. The Pennsylvania court held that it was a violation of due process for one person to represent both the municipality and the hearing board for a variance.[111] Other states, including Iowa and Maine, have also invalidated land-use decisions based on improper *ex parte* communications,[112] but some allow such contact as long as it is disclosed on the record and an opportunity for rebuttal is provided.[113]

---

109.   78 Wash. 2d 858, 480 P.2d 489 (1971). Procedural irregularities were also present in this case, such as denying opponents of the rezoning a right to cross-examine at the hearing. *See also* Smith v. Skagit County, 75 Wash. 2d 715, 453 P.2d 832 (1969).

110.   81 Wash. 2d 312, 501 P.2d 594 (1972). In this case the chairman of the governing board was also the former owner of the applicant company. Further the rezoning was held to be illegal spot zoning.

111.   Horn v. Hilltown, 461 Pa. 745, 337 A.2d 858 (1975).

112.   *See, e.g.,* Rodine v. Zoning Bd. of Adjustment, 434 N.W.2d 124 (Iowa Ct. App. 1988); Mutton Hill Estates v. Town of Oakland, 468 A.2d 989 (Me. 1983).

113.   *See, e.g.,* Barton Contracting Co. v. City of Afton, 268 N.W.2d 712 (Minn. 1978), in which the approval was upheld because the contested communication had also been subsequently made a part of the record. Oregon statutes allow the member receiving an *ex parte* communication to place the substance of the communication on the record and provide for its rebuttal in order to avoid invalidation of the decision. Staff communication with the board is exempt from the *ex parte* rule [OR. REV. STAT. § 227.180(3); applied in Dickas v. City of Beaverton, 92 Or. App. 168, 757 P.2d 451 (1988)]. *See also* King City Water Dist. v. King County Boundary Review Bd., 87 Wash. 2d 536, 554 P.2d 1060 (1976), in which the court held that informal contacts between a board member and staff were permissible unless there was some showing of a partisan benefit.

CHAPTER FOUR

North Carolina Law on Conflicts of Interest

Statutes, Ordinances, and Regulations

North Carolina has no specific state statute addressing the issue of conflict of interest in land-use decisions. However, several general statutory provisions are applicable to certain aspects of the issue. The key statutes, ordinances, codes, and other legal provisions discussed here are set forth in Appendix B.[1]

General Provisions

The state's Administrative Procedure Act governs the conduct of state executive agency decisions.[2] Although not directly applicable to local land-use decisions,[3] these provisions do apply to state-level quasi-judicial hearings. Further the court in Jennewein v. City Council of Wilmington[4] ruled that

---

1. For a more general collection of North Carolina statutes and administrative rules on ethics, see LEGISLATIVE SERVICES OFFICE, NORTH CAROLINA GENERAL ASSEMBLY, ETHICAL CONSIDERATIONS IN STATE GOVERNMENT (March 1988).

2. G.S. 150B-2(1) defines the agencies subject to this law as "any agency, institution, board, commission, bureau, department, division, council, member of the Council of State, or officer of the State government . . . ." It excludes the legislative and judicial branches of state government and does not include city or county agencies.

3. Coastal Ready-Mix Concrete Co. v. Board of Comm'rs, 299 N.C. 620, 265 S.E.2d 379, *reh'g denied,* 300 N.C. 562, 270 S.E.2d 106 (1980).

4. 62 N.C. App. 89, 302 S.E.2d 7, *review denied,* 309 N.C. 461, 307 S.E.2d 365 (1983) (denial of special-use permit in city's historic district).

a similar standard of review should be applied to local land-use decisions.

The Administrative Procedure Act has several provisions requiring fair and unbiased conduct of hearings. G.S. 150B-32(b) provides for the disqualification of an administrative law judge for "personal bias," and G.S. 150B-35 prohibits *ex parte* communication in contested cases. G.S. 150B-40, which applies to occupational licensing agencies, the Department of Insurance, and several banking-related agencies, provides that hearings must be "conducted in a fair and impartial manner," which includes the right to present evidence, the right to cross-examine witnesses, and a prohibition on *ex parte* communications after the notice of the hearing.

The General Assembly has adopted several specific conflict-of-interest provisions for individual boards and commissions. G.S. 143B-283(c) requires that nine of the thirteen members of the Environmental Management Commission be "persons who do not derive any significant portion of their income from persons subject to permits or enforcement orders" under the commission's programs. Also G.S. 143B-282.1(c) provides that no member of the Environmental Management Commission's Committee on Civil Penalty Remissions may hear or vote on a matter in which he or she has an economic interest. G.S. 143-135.28 prohibits members of the State Building Commission from having interests in firms with contracts authorized by the commission. G.S. 143-143.10 requires that the public member of the Manufactured Housing Board have no financial interest in the manufactured-housing industry and that no member participate in any proceeding involving his or her own business. The 1989 General Assembly amended G.S. 113A-104(c) to require that a majority of the members of the Coastal Resources Commission "not derive any significant portion of their income from land development, construction, real estate sales, or lobbying and . . . not otherwise serve as agents for development-related business activities." Further all of the members of the Coastal Resources Commission are directed to "serve and act on the Commission solely for the best interests of the public and the public trust, and . . . bring their particular knowledge and experience to the Commission for that end alone."

At the local level G.S. 160A-511 prohibits members or employees of redevelopment commissions from having any interest, direct or indirect, in property within a redevelopment area, or in a commission's contracts for materials or services.[5] This statute further provides that if a member has held such an interest for at least two years preceding its inclusion in a redevelopment project, the member is to disclose the interest in writing and have it entered in the

---

5. This restriction applies whether the redevelopment authority is being exercised by a separate redevelopment commission, the housing authority, the governing board itself, or any of the other alternative institutional bodies authorized by G.S. Article 22, Chapter 160A.

commission's minutes. Failure to follow the requirements of this statute is declared to be misconduct in office. G.S. 157-5 allows public housing tenants and recipients of housing assistance to serve as members of housing authorities, provided that they not be qualified to vote on matters affecting their official conduct or matters affecting their own individual tenancy, as distinguished from matters affecting tenants in general. G.S.18B-201 addresses conflicts of interest for members of both the state Alcoholic Beverage Control (ABC) Commission and local ABC boards. It prohibits membership on such boards by a person if the person (or a member of the person's household) has a financial interest in any commercial alcoholic beverage enterprise, including any business required to have an ABC permit. The statute provides that exemptions may be granted if "the financial interest in question is so insignificant or remote that it is unlikely to affect the person's official actions in any way." Also a number of local boards have adopted ROBERT'S RULES OF ORDER as a procedural guide. These rules include a general prohibition against conflicts of interest: "No member should vote on a question in which he has a direct personal or pecuniary interest not common to other members of the organization."[6]

Although it is not applicable to citizen boards and land-use decisions, North Carolina does have a general conflict-of-interest statute for legislators that provides insight for a potential approach in the land-use area. The 1975 Legislative Ethics Act[7] primarily takes a disclosure approach to conflicts of interest. Before the adoption of this ethics law, the General Assembly took the position that the electoral process was the best check on conflicts of interest. For example, a 1971 legislative study concluded:

> . . . [T]he Commission is of the opinion that the elective process is the best protection which the public has against abuse by a legislator who by his votes and activities clearly works for a selfish private interest and against clear public interest. The election campaign occurs every two years. Charges that a legislator has allowed private interest to outweigh the public interest can, and in the light of past experience will, be made against incumbents. Properly presented, these charges present an issue not as to the honesty or integrity of the legislator, but as to his suitability for the office of legislator—Does he represent too narrow a segment of the electorate?[8]

---

6. ROBERT'S RULES OF ORDER NEWLY REVISED § 44 (1970).

7. G.S. Art. 14, Ch. 120. North Carolina also has a campaign finance law that, among other provisions, sets contribution limits and requires reporting of contributions [G.S. Art. 22A, Ch. 163].

8. *Legislative Ethics 7*, in 1971 REPORTS OF THE LEGISLATIVE RESEARCH COMMISSION. On this issue generally, see COMMITTEE ON LEGISLATIVE RULES, NATIONAL LEGISLATIVE CONFERENCE, CONFLICT OF INTEREST AND RELATED REGULATIONS FOR STATE LEGISLATURES (1971). There is a substantial body of literature on public financial disclosure requirements. *See, e.g.*, Note, *Constitutionality of Financial Disclosure Laws*, 59 CORNELL L. REV. 345 (1974).

However, later observers argued that electoral review alone was insufficient. In advocating a new ethics statute, Legislative Services Officer Clyde Ball in 1975 contended that ethics statutes "should be aimed at . . . the less-than-criminal but nevertheless improper influence that special interests or the legislator's own private interest may exert upon his decisions as a legislator."[9] Ball proposed a preelection disclosure of interests as the appropriate approach, distinguishing between quasi-judicial and legislative decisions thus:

> The courts have traditionally sought to have individual cases decided by jurors who have no knowledge of the case, except what comes to them through the judicial process. However valuable such ignorance is in the judicial process, it is not conducive to good legislative results. If a district knows the financial and professional connections of a citizen and elects him to a seat in the General Assembly, he should be allowed to participate in the full range of legislative activity.[10]

The 1975 legislation that was enacted includes several provisions. G.S. 120-89 requires candidates for the General Assembly to file statements of economic interest, and G.S. 120-95 requires the same of all members of the General Assembly. These statements, which become public records, generally must disclose all financial interests in excess of $5,000 (G.S. 120-96). G.S. 120-88 requires legislators to disqualify themselves from taking any action to further their own economic interests when they conclude that they will be unable to exercise independent judgment. The law also establishes a Legislative Ethics Committee that sets the form for disclosure statements, lists ethical principles and guidelines, suggests rules of conduct, and investigates alleged violations of the law. G.S. 120-103 provides that if the committee determines a violation to exist, the matter may be referred to the Attorney General for prosecution and may also be referred to the appropriate house of the General Assembly, which may censure, suspend, or expel the offending member.

The North Carolina Code of Judicial Conduct includes a standard that judges use to determine whether they should hear a matter when there may be a conflict of interest.[11] This standard may serve as a particularly useful guide when

---

9. Ball, *Legislative Ethics: Ends and Means,* 40 POPULAR GOV'T 18, 22 (Spring 1975).

10. *Id.* at 22–26. Of course, most citizen board members dealing with land-use issues are not elected.

11. The New Jersey courts have ruled that because zoning boards of adjustment exercise quasi-judicial power, these canons are a relevant guide for them [McVoy v. Bd. of Adjustment, 213 N.J. Super. 109, 516 A.2d 634 (1986)].

The North Carolina State Bar's Rules of Professional Conduct are also instructive in this respect. Rule 8.1, Action as a Public Official, provides:

citizen bodies are acting in a quasi-judicial fashion. Canon 3(C) of the code provides that judges should disqualify themselves in any proceeding in which their impartiality might reasonably be questioned, including but not limited to situations in which they have a personal bias or prejudice, they have personal knowledge of disputed facts, they or an immediate family member has a financial interest in the matter that could be substantially affected by the outcome, they are closely related to an interested party, or they have previously served (or have a law partner who has served) as a lawyer or a witness in the matter. Canon 3(D) of the code allows a judge who would otherwise be disqualified because of his or her potential financial interest or relation to a party, to disclose that fact, and if all parties then agree in writing that the financial interest is insubstantial or the relationship is immaterial, the judge may continue to hear the matter.[12] This waiver may not be applied if the disqualification is based on personal bias or prejudice or on the judge's prior service as an attorney for one of the parties.

Criminal Laws

Bribery of public officials is clearly illegal. G.S. 14-217 makes it a felony for an office holder to receive ". . . directly or indirectly, anything of value or personal advantage, or the promise thereof, for performing or omitting to perform any official act. . . ." G.S. 14-218 makes the offering of such a bribe a felony.[13] North Carolina also has prohibitions against citizen board members

---

A lawyer who holds public office shall not:

(A) Use his public position to obtain, or attempt to obtain, a special advantage in legislative matters for himself, or for a client under circumstances where he knows or it is obvious that such action is not in the public interest.

(B) Use his public position to influence, or attempt to influence, a tribunal to act in favor of himself or his client.

(C) Accept anything of value from any person when the lawyer knows or it is obvious that the offer is for the purpose of influencing his action as a public official.

12. *But see* McVoy v. Bd. of Adjustment, 213 N.J. Super. 109, 516 A.2d 634 (1986). This case involved members of a zoning board of adjustment who belonged to a church seeking a variance and who were therefore disqualified. The court ruled that when an impermissible conflict of interest exists, disclosing that fact and securing the approval of those at a quasi-judicial variance hearing to continued participation is not permissible. To avoid the appearance of unfairness, nonparticipation is required and cannot be waived.

13. North Carolina also has statutes prohibiting gifts and favors to those involved in contracting and in inspecting or supervising construction [G.S. 133-32]. Other specialized statutes apply to school and transportation officials [G.S. 14-236, 136-13, 136-14].

having direct financial relations with the government body they are serving.[14]
Finally state law provides that a state or local official who willfully fails to discharge
any legally required duty is guilty of a misdemeanor.[15] This latter statute does not
impose criminal liability for an official's error in judgment. However, in the conflict-of-interest area this statute could apply to situations in which an official
purposely deleted relevant information from a required financial disclosure statement, and it could cover a situation in which an official continued to participate
in a decision after being advised to withdraw because of a conflict of interest.

Voting Statutes

North Carolina has statutes that specifically address the question of when
local elected officials may be excused from voting because of a conflict of interest.
These statutes are relatively narrowly drawn. They address only financial conflicts,
they apply only to elected boards, and they cover only personal conflicts of the
member.

For city councils G.S. 160A-75 provides, "No member shall be excused
from voting except upon matters involving the consideration of his own financial

---

14.   G.S. 14-234. *See* Wicker, *Conflict of Interest and Self-Dealing in North Carolina*, Popular Gov't (Winter 1980). *See also* R. Anderson, American Law of Zoning §
19.19 (3d ed. 1990); Kaplan and Lillich, *Municipal Conflicts of Interest: Inconsistencies
and Patchwork Prohibitions*, 58 Colum. L. Rev. 157 (1958). Several North Carolina
local charters elaborate upon this basic financial self-dealing prohibition. *See, e.g.*, the town
charter update for Kernersville [1989 N.C. Sess. Laws ch. 381, § 23].

North Carolina courts have held a variety of financial arrangements between local
governments and their board members to be illegal under this statute, though in a number
of instances the statute has subsequently been amended to allow certain of these activities.
See Snipes v. City of Winston, 126 N.C. 374, 35 S.E. 610 (1900) (city hiring council
member invalid); Davidson v. Guilford County, 152 N.C. 436, 67 S.E. 918 (1910)
(compensation of county board member for county work invalid; court ruled that this
conclusion against self-interest could be reached independently of statute); King v.
Guilford County, 152 N.C. 438, 67 S.E. 919 (1910) (compensation of county highway
chairman for county work invalid); State v. Williams, 153 N.C. 595, 68 S.E. 900 (1910)
(council member contract with city invalid, even though member did not vote on contract); Carolina Beach v. Mintz, 212 N.C. 578, 194 S.E. 309 (1937) (reimbursement of
council-member staff work invalid); and Lexington Insulation Co. v. Davidson County,
243 N.C. 252, 90 S.E.2d 496 (1955) (contract with board member's company invalid
and *quantum meruit* recovery not allowed for contracts in violation of statute). The courts
have allowed contracts with a member's employer, however. *See* State v. Weddell, 153
N.C. 587, 68 S.E. 897 (1910); State v. Debnam, 196 N.C. 740, 146 S.E. 857 (1929)
(purchase of truck from company that was owned by wife of board member and that
employed board member did not violate statute).

15.   G.S. 14-230.

interest or official conduct." In such cases the board member may be excused only by a majority vote of the council.[16] If not excused, the board member is automatically recorded as voting in the affirmative if he or she is present but not actually casting a vote.[17] G.S. 153A-44 contains a similar provision for county boards of commissioners. These statutes apply only to local elected officials and do not affect voting by members of planning boards, boards of adjustment, or state citizen commissions. The statutes ensure that a quorum can be maintained and that the public's business will not be delayed by members seeking to avoid controversial votes.

The voting statutes, by specifically allowing governing board members to be excused in matters involving their own financial interest, emphasize the prohibition against financial self-dealing and financial conflicts of interest. However, they pose a dilemma for elected officials in local governments that have chosen to retain quasi-judicial decision-making authority at the council and commission levels. When voting on a special-use permit after an adjudicatory hearing, a board member may need to be excused from participation because of a nonfinancial conflict (e.g., because he or she is closely related to one of the parties). However, the statute on its face allows board members to be excused only for financial conflicts.

The city of Charlotte has secured local legislation to amend the voting statute to address one aspect of balancing the need to require elected officials to vote

---

16. The statute does not address the question of whether only a member with a potential conflict of interest may raise the matter or whether any member may move to exclude another because of a conflict. As with other provisions regarding the qualifications of a member to vote, this would seem to be a germane issue that could be raised by any member. Given the needs to produce a fair decision and to avoid rehearing matters and given the potential monetary damages that could result from improper participation of a single member (see the discussion of the *Crump* decision effects *infra* pp. 51–53), provisions should be made to resolve questions of disqualification as early in the decision-making process as possible. It further seems reasonable that disputes should be resolved by a majority of the board, but this consideration must be tempered with concern for not allowing a duly elected or appointed board member to be lightly disqualified over his or her objection. It would be prudent to include explicit provisions, either by statute, ordinance, or by-law, that clearly established how a question of disqualification might be raised, when it might or must be done, by whom, and who would decide the question if it was disputed. See the model ordinance in the appendix for an example.

17. An interesting situation arises if a board member declares a conflict of interest but the full board refuses to vote to excuse him or her from voting. If the person thereafter votes, the action taken is subject to challenge because of improper participation. If the person was to abstain from voting and his or her vote was automatically counted as an affirmative vote by action of this statute, this would have the same practical effect as improper participation and still subject the action taken to challenge because of improper participation.

with the need to ensure protection of due process rights in quasi-judicial land-use decisions. The Charlotte city code provides that a council member must vote except on matters involving his or her own official conduct, his or her financial interest, "or when the member failed to attend the entire hearing for the issuance of a special use permit."[18] This provision ensures that only board members who have heard all of the evidence at a hearing take part in the decision.

The constitutional guarantees for due process in a quasi-judicial hearing should take precedence over the statutory mandates regarding voting, thereby allowing recusal of a governing board member who has a nonfinancial conflict of interest. However, this will remain an uncertain area of the law until the conflicting legal obligations are resolved by the courts or the legislature.

If a member of a citizen board is disqualified for bias or conflict of interest, a question is raised as to the impact on securing a quorum or an extraordinary majority, such as a three-fourths vote that may be required to approve a land-use matter.[19] Municipal boards of adjustment may grant variances, special exceptions, and conditional- and special-use permits or otherwise decide in favor of an applicant only on "the concurring votes of four-fifths of the members of the board."[20] The county statute uses the phrase "by a vote of four-fifths of [the board of adjustment's] members."[21] In another instance of an extraordinary majority being required, city governing boards may adopt a rezoning when a valid protest petition has been filed only on the "favorable vote of three fourths of all the members of the city council."[22] Because these various statutes explicitly refer to "members" of the board rather than to those present and voting, some commentators have concluded that the required majorities should not be reduced by any disqualifications due to conflicts of interest or bias.[23] For boards of

---

18. Section 3-23 of the Charlotte charter, authorized by 1984 Sess. Laws ch. 1008. Similarly, see Howard County v. Bay Harvestore Sys., 60 Md. App. 19, 478 A.2d 1172 (1984), in which it was ruled that zoning board members who were not present at the hearing on a rezoning could not participate in the decision.

19. *See generally* Annotation, *What Constitutes Requisite Majority of Members of Municipal Council Voting on Issue,* 43 A.L.R.2d 698 (1955); Annotation, *Abstention from Voting of Member of Municipal Council Present at a Session as Affecting Requisite Voting Majority,* 63 A.L.R. 3d 1072 (1975).

20. G.S. 160A-388(e). This four-fifths rule applies only to boards of adjustment and to plannings boards acting as boards of adjustment. G.S. 160A-381 provides that if a governing board is issuing a special- or conditional-use permit, only a simple majority is required. G.S. 153A-340 establishes the same rule for county boards of adjustment.

21. G.S. 153A-345(e).

22. G.S. 160A-385(a).

23. M. BROUGH AND P. GREEN, THE ZONING BOARD OF ADJUSTMENT IN NORTH CAROLINA 47 (1984).

adjustment this can be addressed by having alternate members, but that solution is not possible for governing boards.

The lack of a quorum or enough qualified voting members for required extraordinary majorities results in either automatic denial or action under a common law rule of necessity.[24] Absent a statute explicitly providing for resolution of this question,[25] courts addressing the issue in a land-use context have split on the question of whether a disqualified member's seat should be considered vacant for the purposes of the matter.

In Aurentz v. Planning Board of Little Egg Harbor Township,[26] a seven-member planning board in New Jersey was reviewing a subdivision plat. Three of the members worked for either the applicant or the contractors who would be involved in construction of the subdivision if it was approved. One additional member was absent from the meeting. The court held that the three members properly abstained, leaving only three qualified members present; therefore there was no quorum and no valid approval. On the other hand a Texas court ruled that when a statute required the favorable vote of three-fourths of "all the members of the legislative body," the seat of a member disqualified for conflict of interest should be considered vacant and not counted in computing the number of votes required.[27]

---

24. *See* Jarrott v. Scrivener, 225 F. Supp. 827 (D.D.C. 1964). Malone v. City of Poway, 746 F.2d 1375 (9th Cir. 1984), involved an action brought under 42 U.S.C. § 1983 charging deprivation of civil rights based on allegedly prejudiced governing board members not disqualifying themselves in the consideration of a special-use permit. The court ruled that because the city council was the only body with the power to issue the permit, the rule of necessity imposed a duty on the council to consider the application. *See also* Gonsalves v. City of Dairy Valley, 265 Cal. App. 2d 400, 71 Cal. Rptr. 255 (1968).

25. For example, Colorado's statute on voting by municipal board members requires disqualification if a member has a personal or private interest in a matter. The statute goes on, however, to provide that a member with such a conflict may vote "if his participation is necessary to obtain a quorum or otherwise enable the body to act and if he complies with the voluntary disclosure provisions" of the law [COLO. REV. STAT. § 31-4-404(3)].

26. 171 N.J. Super. 135, 408 A.2d 140 (Law Div. 1979). *See also* Low v. Town of Madison, 135 Conn. 1, 60 A.2d 774 (1948). In this case a protest petition had been filed by neighbors, so a unanimous vote by the board was required. The court ruled that this did not authorize the husband's participation because his wife could defer her petition until he was no longer on the board, or if there was greater urgency to her petition, he could resign from the board.

27. Hannan v. City of Coppell, 583 S.W.2d 817 (Tex. Civ. App. 1979); Alamo Heights v. Gerety, 264 S.W.2d 778 (Tex. Civ. App. 1954). *See also* Croaff v. Evans, 130 Ariz. 353, 636 P.2d 131 (App. 1981); Meixell v. Hellertown Borough Council, 370 Pa. 420, 88 A.2d 594 (1952).

The general law in North Carolina is that a majority of the members of a board constitute a quorum,[28] and absent a statute providing otherwise, when vacancies reduce a board's membership below the number needed for a quorum, the board cannot perform its corporate functions.[29] Although North Carolina courts have not addressed this issue in a conflict-of-interest context, they have ruled that a seat that is vacant by reason of resignation should not be counted in computing the required affirmative votes under a city charter provision calling for a three-fourths vote "of the entire board" in order to issue bonds.[30] Also G.S. 160A-74 provides that vacant seats are not counted toward a city council's membership in establishing a quorum, and G.S. 160A-75 provides that the seats of those excused from voting shall not be considered when computing the majority needed for a city to adopt an ordinance or to enter into a contract.[31] It would be reasonable to treat all disqualifications due to bias or conflicts of interest the same way, but until the voting statutes are clarified or the court interprets them, this also remains an uncertain area of the law.[32]

---

28. Hill v. Ponder, 221 N.C. 58, 19 S.E.2d 5 (1942).

29. Edwards v. Bd. of Education, 235 N.C. 345, 70 S.E.2d 170 (1952). In this case two of three members of a board of education were deemed to have vacated their seats because of a violation of the prohibition against dual-office holding (which has subsequently been liberalized). The court noted that an expeditious statutory process was available to fill vacancies "in order to obviate the legal paralysis incident to such an eventuality." Of course, such an expeditious process does not exist when the "vacancy" in an elected board's membership is a temporary one due to a conflict of interest.

30. Comm'rs of Town of Salem v. Wachovia Loan & Trust Co., 143 N.C. 110, 55 S.E. 442 (1906). The court ruled that use of the phrase "of the entire board" meant the board in existence at the time (thereby excluding vacancies), as distinguished from use of the term "of the entire board elected," which would not exclude vacancies. Because the land-use voting statutes similarly refer to "members of the board," "its members," and "all the members," they would seem to be included within the rationale of this case.

31. The county standard in G.S. 153A-43 provides that a majority of the membership of a board constitute a quorum and the number required for a quorum is *not* affected by vacancies. G.S 153A-45 requires a majority of votes cast, a quorum being present, to adopt an ordinance.

32. An alternative interpretation rendering the same result would be to consider a member who is temporarily excused from participation because of a conflict of interest as present for quorum purposes in order to allow meetings to continue without disruption in the face of a fluctuating number of voting members. G.S. 160A-74 explicitly takes this approach for members who are absent without excuse. However, additional statutory clarification is needed to address the question of the impact of a disqualification due to a conflict of interest on the extraordinary majorities required for boards of adjustment and for protest petitions. Under the rationale of Comm'rs of Town of Salem v. Wachovia Loan & Trust Co., 143 N.C. 110, 55 S.E. 442 (1906), vacancies reduce the size of a board and consequently the number of votes needed for a four-fifths or three-fourths

Executive Order

Financial disclosure requirements and a conflict-of-interest prohibition for state policy-making employees and citizen members of state boards, commissions, and councils have been in effect since 1977.[33] The executive order creating these requirements notes that "public office in North Carolina must always be regarded as a public trust" and that the people "have a fundamental right to the assurance that officers of their government will not use their public position for personal gain." The order prohibits those subject to it from engaging in "any activity which interferes or is in conflict with the proper and effective discharge of such person's official duties." The order also requires the annual submission of a detailed statement of economic interest that includes a list of all assets, liabilities, and income over $5,000 and a list of gifts valued at more than $100 (over $50 if the donor has any business with or is regulated by the state). The statement is reviewed by the State Board of Ethics for conflicts of interest, and the board may recommend

---

majority. However, if the intent of the legislature is to allow these types of decisions only when the extraordinary majority of the board *includes* those not voting because of a conflict of interest, the statutes at G.S 153A-345(e), 160A-385(a), and 160A-388(e) need to be clarified to require such.

33.   Exec. Order No. 1, January 31, 1985. A similar executive order issued by Governor James Hunt was effective from 1977 to 1985 [Exec. Order No. 1, January 10, 1977].

Another example of a specialized provision prohibiting financial conflicts of interest is Exec. Order No. VI, issued by Governor James Holshouser on August 20, 1974. This order required that at least five members of the Environmental Management Commission not receive a significant portion (10 percent) of their income from water-pollution-discharge permittees or applicants. This is now required by both federal and state law. *See* 40 C.F.R. 123.25(c) and G.S. 143B-283(c).

State government has also employed educational efforts to stress avoidance of conflicts of interest. For example, in November 1989 Secretary William Cobey distributed a flyer on this topic to all employees of the Department of Environment, Health, and Natural Resources. The notice referenced the state constitutional provision to take care that the laws be faithfully executed and advised these employees:

> Each of us must refrain from any official act that would advance our personal welfare or appear to do so. Even the appearance of impropriety can undermine the confidence and respect of the citizens for whom we work. . . . By applying proper ethical standards at all times, we will continue to earn the trust and respect of the public we serve.

For similar disclosure requirements for federal government officials, see Financial Disclosure Requirements of Federal Personnel, 5 U.S.C.A. app. 6 (West Supp. 1990). *See also* Exec. Order No. 11222, 30 Fed. Reg. 6469 (1965), as amended by Exec. Order No. 14590, 36 Fed. Reg. 7831 (1971), for federal executive orders on this subject.

remedial action if actual or potential conflicts are identified.[34] The board also investigates complaints regarding conflicts of interest and provides for public inspection of the statements of economic interest.

Local Codes

Several local governments also have codes of ethics regarding conflicts of interest. The North Carolina League of Municipalities conducted a survey in late 1989 of ordinances adopted by North Carolina cities.[35] It received responses from 278 of the 510 municipalities. Thirty-two municipalities (11.5 percent) reported that they had adopted ethics guidelines for boards and elected officials.[36] Given that over 350 North Carolina municipalities have zoning ordinances, a vast majority are exercising this power without the assistance of express ethics guidelines.[37]

The most common local code requirement is for financial disclosure statements, mandated, for example, by Guilford and Orange counties, Greensboro, Charlotte, and Chapel Hill. Orange County commissioners must disclose (for both themselves and their spouses) all real property holdings within the county and interests in firms doing business with the county.[38] In addition to disclosure

---

34. Interpretive Memorandum No. 1 was issued by the North Carolina Board of Ethics on April 5, 1985, to define "actual" and "potential" conflicts of interest. Actual conflicts are those whose very existence creates a conflict, such as a utility manager's serving on the utilities commission. Potential conflicts are situations in which a member may make decisions to benefit his or her personal interest, such as voting on regulations governing his or her business. The memo states that the Board of Ethics will generally recommend remedial action (such as divestiture) for actual conflicts. For potential conflicts members are advised to disclose the financial interest and disqualify themselves from voting on or discussing any matter that could affect private interests.

35. NORTH CAROLINA LEAGUE OF MUNICIPALITIES, RESULTS OF THE 1989 MUNICIPAL ORDINANCE SURVEY (Jan. 17, 1990).

36. The thirty-two municipalities reporting adoption of ethics ordinances included, in order of descending population, Charlotte, Raleigh, Fayetteville, Wilmington, Chapel Hill, Hickory, Asheboro, Morganton, Waynesville, Benson, Wallace, Lowell, Scotland Neck, Liberty, Bethel, Sharpsburg, Kenly, Rutherford College, Holly Springs, Norlina, Pikeville, Montreat, Catawba, Bolton, Elk Park, Grimesland, Simpson, East Arcadia, Turkey, Beech Mountain, Halifax, and Sims.

37. A 1985 survey by the Division of Community Assistance, Department of Natural Resources and Community Development, indicated that 349 of the 495 municipalities existing at that time, some 71 percent, had adopted zoning ordinances. Several additional municipalities have adopted zoning since that survey.

38. 1987 Sess. Laws ch. 460, tit. VII. Chapel Hill was authorized to require similar disclosures and to prohibit council members from voting on matters involving their property or business interests [1989 Sess. Laws ch. 478, § 4]. Article III

the Guilford County code specifically requires a county commissioner to disqualify himself or herself from voting on any matter involving a disclosed interest.[39] The Greensboro code states, "No member of any board or commission may discuss, advocate or vote on any matter in which he has a separate, private or monetary interest, either direct or indirect."[40]

In each of these instances the local government involved has removed any question about its statutory authority to adopt such requirements by securing local legislation authorizing an ordinance.

Case Law

Although there have been no reported cases directly on the subject of conflicts of interest in land-use decisions, North Carolina does have a substantial body of case law on the general issue of bias and conflict of interest in governmental and judicial decision making. These cases are particularly helpful in establishing the law for addressing conflicts of interest in quasi-judicial land-use decisions.

General Standards

In an early case involving the propriety of a clerk of court ruling on the acceptability for recordation of his own mortgage, the court in 1890 in White v. Connelly[41] adopted the English common law prohibiting a person from acting as a judge in his or her own case. The court emphasized the necessity of avoiding even the appearance of conflicts of interest, quoting an 1852 English case:

> This maxim applies in all cases where judicial functions are to be exercised, and excludes all who are interested, however remotely, from taking part in their exercise.
>
> It is not left to the discretion of a Judge, or to his sense of decency, to decide whether he shall act or not; all his powers are subject to this absolute limitation; and when his own rights are in question, he has no authority to determine the cause. . . . [T]he maxim "no man is to be a judge in his own cause," should be held sacred. And that is not to be confined to a cause in which he is a party, but applies to a cause in which he has an interest.

---

of the Charlotte code contains the code of ethics for the mayor, council members, and key appointed staff.

39. The Guilford County provision is § 1-55 of its code [1973 Sess. Laws ch. 296, § 5].

40. Greensboro Code § 2-142. Other city codes state the requirement in more general terms, such as the Durham provision that officials "fairly and impartially perform the duties of their office."

41. 105 N.C. 65, 11 S.E. 177 (1890).

[Those involved should] take care not only that in their decrees they are not influenced by their personal interest, but to avoid the appearance of laboring under such an influence.[42]

In the 1951 case, Ponder v. Davis,[43] the court noted the importance of avoiding even the appearance of bias in order to preserve public confidence in the judicial system, ruling, "It is not enough for a judge to be just in his judgments; he should strive to make the parties and the community feel that he is just; he owes this to himself, to the law and to the position he holds."[44] The court also quoted with approval several other states' similar rulings:

> The purity and integrity of the judicial process ought to be protected against any taint of suspicion to the end that the public and litigants may have the highest confidence in the integrity and fairness of the courts.[45]

> It is but the utterance of a legal platitude to say that it is of the utmost importance that every man should have a fair and impartial trial of his case . . . . But we go further and say that it is also important that every man should know he has had a fair and impartial trial; or, at least, that he should have no just ground for the suspicion that he has not had such a trial.[46]

A more recent statement of this general principle is found in a 1984 condemnation case, Colonial Pipeline Co. v. Weaver,[47] in which the court ruled, "[I]t is axiomatic, of course, that it is the lawful right of every litigant to expect utter impartiality and neutrality in the judge who tries his case . . . . This right can neither be denied nor abridged."[48]

---

42. *Id.* at 70, 11 S.E. at 179. *See also* Trenwith v. Smallwood, 111 N.C. 132, 15 S.E. 1030 (1892); Long v. Crews, 113 N.C. 256, 18 S.E. 499 (1893); Scranton and N. C. Land and Lumber Co. v. Jennett, 128 N.C. 3, 37 S.E. 954 (1901); Edwards v. Sutton, 185 N.C. 102, 116 S.E. 163 (1923) (division of estate by person interested in outcome void); Cowan v. Dale, 189 N.C. 684, 128 S.E. 155 (1925) (probate of mortgage by mortgagee void); Norman v. Branch Banking and Trust, 193 N.C. 791, 138 S.E. 162 (1927) (clerk of court may not admit deed of trust to probate where he or she is mortgagee).

The rule involved in the *White* case is now codified at G.S. 7A-104.

43. 233 N.C. 699, 65 S.E.2d 356 (1951).

44. *Id.* at 706.

45. Haslam v. Morrison, 113 Utah 14, 20, 190 P.2d 520, 523 (1948).

46. Kentucky Journal Publishing Co. v. Gaines, 139 Ky. 747, 758, 110 S.W. 268, 272 (1908).

47. 310 N.C. 93, 310 S.E.2d 338 (1984).

48. *Id.* at 103, 310 S.E.2d at 344. *See also* Russell v. Town of Morehead City, 90 N.C. App. 675, 370 S.E.2d 56 (1988), in which the court ruled that the expression of an opinion by a judge during a jury trial unfairly prejudiced the jury and warranted a new trial.

Financial Conflicts of Interest

North Carolina courts have established a strong standard prohibiting any direct financial conflicts of interest in both legislative and judicial decision making. The North Carolina courts have long ruled that governmental decision makers should not participate in deciding legislative matters in which they have a pecuniary interest. In Kendall v. Stafford,[49] a 1919 case involving the authority of the Greensboro city council members to vote themselves a raise, the court ruled:

> The public policy of the State, found in the statutes and judicial decisions, has been pronounced against permitting one to sit in judgment on his own cause, or to act on a matter affecting the public when he has a direct pecuniary interest, and this is a principle of the common law which has existed for hundreds of years.[50]

Subsequent statutory amendments now allow city councils to set their members' salaries.[51] In a case involving legislators voting on their own travel expenses, *In re* Advisory Opinion re Constitutionality of HB 276,[52] the court in 1947 ruled, "It has long been a rule of general observance that self-interest disqualifies one from acting in a public capacity where unbiased judgment is required."[53]

The court has generally required a direct and substantial financial conflict to invalidate a legislative decision. An example is the series of cases involving challenges to school-location decisions by local boards of education. In Venable v. School Committee of Pilot Mountain,[54] the general rule was set forth: "The courts are astute to impeach and invalidate any transaction where an official has any personal interest whatever in the matter decided by him. The very 'appearance of evil' must be avoided."[55] The court went on to recognize, however, that such legislative decisions were vested in the sound discretion of the board and were

---

49. 178 N.C. 461, 101 S.E. 15 (1919).

50. *Id.* at 464, 101 S.E. at 16.

51. G.S. 160A-64.

52. 227 N.C. 705, 41 S.E.2d 749 (1947).

53. *Id.* at 707, 41 S.E.2d at 750. Although statutory provisions such as those on voting (G.S. 160A-75 and G.S. 153A-44) and those on financial contracts between a board member and his or her government body (G.S. 14-234) are important guides to the limits of legally acceptable conduct, the courts also look to constitutional and common law limitations. For example, the court noted in Davidson v. Guilford County, "Independently of any statute or precedent, upon general principles of law and morality, a member of an official board cannot contract with the body of which he is a member. To permit it would open the door wide to fraud and corruption" [152 N.C. 436, 437, 67 S.E. 918, 919 (1910)].

54. 149 N.C. 120, 62 S.E. 902 (1908).

55. *Id.* at 122, 62 S.E. at 903.

not to be overturned by the judiciary in the absence of a clear showing of misconduct or improper motives. In the *Venable* case it was held that contributions to the purchase price of a new school site by one board member and the brothers of two other board members did not constitute a conflict of interest. In a subsequent case, Kistler v. Board of Education of Randolph County,[56] the court held that ownership of nearby property that might be enhanced in value (as opposed to a financial interest in the site itself) did not constitute a conflict of interest absent an allegation that the member exercised an "improper or corrupt influence" over other board members. To establish such an abuse of discretion, a direct personal financial conflict is required.[57]

These cases evidence a general judicial policy in North Carolina against allowing people with a direct and substantial financial conflict of interest in the outcome of a legislative governmental decision to participate in that decision. With judicial and quasi-judicial decisions avoidance of even the appearance of a financial conflict of interest is required.

Prejudgment

The question of prejudgment on the merits of a matter that is to be decided in a judicial or quasi-judicial manner has been addressed on several occasions by the court. Most of these cases involve judicial recusation in criminal cases. G.S. 15A-1223(a) provides for disqualification of a judge in a criminal proceeding if he or she is prejudiced against the moving party or in favor of the adverse party, is closely related to the defendant, or is for any other reason unable to perform his or her duties in an impartial manner. The oath of office for judges, set forth in G.S. 11-11, further provides that judges "will administer justice without favoritism to anyone" and will "faithfully and impartially discharge" their duties.

The test set by the courts in these cases to determine whether a judge should participate in a matter is that he or she should be excused if a reasonable person knowing all the circumstances would have doubts about the individual's ability to rule impartially. Several North Carolina cases have applied this test to mandate nonparticipation. In McClendon v. Clinard[58] the Court of Appeals ruled that a judge should be recused from further consideration of a case after initiating a

---

56.　233 N.C. 400, 64 S.E.2d 403 (1951).

57.　In a similar line of cases, the courts have ruled that site-selection decisions by public housing authorities may be overturned only if shown to be arbitrary or capricious or an abuse of discretion. A showing of malice, fraud, or bad faith is not required [*In re* Hous. Auth., 235 N.C. 463, 70 S.E.2d 500 (1952); Philbrook v. Chapel Hill Hous. Auth., 269 N.C. 598, 153 S.E.2d 153 (1967)].

58.　38 N.C. App. 353, 247 S.E.2d 783 (1978).

disciplinary complaint regarding an attorney's contact with a potential juror. In State v. Hill[59] the Court of Appeals ruled that a judge should refer a decision on a recusal motion to another judge when he had previously expressed a view that the defendant had implicated himself while testifying in another trial. The North Carolina Supreme Court in State v. Fie[60] ruled that the appearance of a predisposition was sufficient to warrant recusal.

In other cases no prejudicial bias was found. The court ruled in State v. Poole[61] that a vague allegation of prejudice was insufficient to warrant recusal. The Court of Appeals has also addressed the issue in a series of cases. In Love v. Pressley[62] a trial judge's having made adverse findings of fact regarding a party in a previous trial was held not to constitute bias. In In re Smith[63] the court found that there was no requirement to be recused in a contempt proceeding when no bias or prejudice had been shown, the alleged contempt had not involved the personal feelings of the judge, and the proceedings had been conducted in a calm, detached judicial manner. In State v. Duvall[64] the court ruled that presiding over a prior trial of a codefendant did not constitute bias absent some showing of personal interest.

A 1990 case presents an interesting parallel to the issue of bias in quasi-judicial land-use decisions. This case, Crump v. Board of Education,[65] involved a dismissed teacher's claim that the school board was biased against him and that this prejudgment violated his constitutional rights.[66] The teacher's dismissal had been upheld in a previous case,[67] so the only issue in this case was whether the hearing had been fair and whether monetary damages could be awarded solely on the basis of unfairness. The trial court found the hearing to have been unfair because at least one member of the school board had obtained knowledge of the

---

59. 45 N.C. App. 136, 263 S.E.2d 14, *review denied*, 300 N.C. 377 (1980). *See also* State v. Crabtree, 66 N.C. App. 662, 312 S.E.2d 219 (1984).

60. 320 N.C. 626, 359 S.E.2d 774 (1984).

61. 305 N.C. 308, 289 S.E.2d 335 (1982) (criminal defendant's allegation that judge had remarked that he "wasn't going to protect criminals" was held not to be grounds for recusal).

62. 34 N.C. App. 503, 239 S.E.2d 574 (1977), *review denied*, 294 N.C. 441, 241 S.E.2d 843 (1978).

63. 45 N.C. App. 123, 263 S.E.2d 23 (1980), *rev'd on other grounds*, 301 N.C. 621, 272 S.E.2d 834 (1981).

64. 50 N.C. App. 684, 275 S.E.2d 842, *rev'd on other grounds*, 304 N.C. 557, 284 S.E.2d 495 (1981).

65. 326 N.C. 603, 392 S.E.2d 579 (1990).

66. The claim for damages was brought under 42 U.S.C.A. § 1983 (West 1981).

67. 79 N.C. App. 372, 339 S.E.2d 483, *disc. review denied*, 317 N.C. 333, 346 S.E.2d 137 (1986).

matter before the hearing but had denied that knowledge at the hearing.[68] A jury awarded the dismissed teacher $78,000 in damages because of the biased hearing, and the court upheld that award.

The court in the *Crump* case recognized the inherent tension between the need to secure knowledgeable citizens to serve on boards and the necessity of having impartial decision makers for quasi-judicial decisions. The court noted:

> Members of a school board are expected to be knowledgeable about school-related activities in their district. Board members will sometimes have discussed certain issues that later become the subject of board deliberations; such knowledge and discussions are inevitable aspects of their multi-faceted roles as administrators, investigators and adjudicators. However, when performing their quasi-judicial function during a board hearing and any resulting deliberations, members must be able to set aside their prior knowledge and preconceptions concerning the matter at issue, and base their considerations solely upon the evidence adduced at the hearing.[69]

The court went on to hold that if a single board member had a predetermined opinion that was fixed and not susceptible to change, that member should not participate at all in the quasi-judicial hearing:

> A critical component of any quasi-judicial hearing and decision-making by a deliberative body is the give and take which occurs when group members share their observations and opinions. There is a fundamental notion that each member will enter the hearing with an open mind, listen to and view the evidence, share his or her observations, analyses and opinions with the other board members, listen to the other members' comments, and only then finally commit to a vote. One biased member can skew the entire process by what he or she does, or does not do, during the hearing and deliberations.[70]

Therefore in the *Crump* case the court ruled that (1) prejudgment constituted impermissible bias in a quasi-judicial matter; (2) participation by one biased member violated the rights of those at the hearing, even if that member's vote

---

68.   This denial was a critical factor in the finding of bias. As the court concluded:

In this case, the cost of the procedure which we conclude due process required was whatever it would have taken for one or more Board members to candidly answer Crump's questions about their pre-hearing knowledge. The injury to Crump from being forced to participate in a hearing that the jury in this case determined was unfair, on the other hand, was valued by the Catawba County jury at $78,000. It should not cost that much to be candid; talk is cheap. [326 N.C. at 625.]

69.   326 N.C. at 616–17.
70.   326 N.C. at 619–20.

was not needed for a majority; and (3) even if the substantive decision at the hearing was correct (in this instance the dismissal of the teacher was held to be correct), if the right to a fair hearing was violated, that alone could justify awarding monetary damages.

Association with the Parties

North Carolina courts have also ruled that a person should not participate in a quasi-judicial decision if he or she has too close an association with the parties involved. In 1927 the court ruled in State v. Hartley[71] that a judge who was related to the prosecuting witness in a libel suit should recuse himself. In 1951 the court decided in Ponder v. Davis that a judge who had campaigned for a sheriff should not hear legal actions challenging the sheriff's election, ruling that a judge should recuse himself or herself in proceedings "where they involve personal feelings which do not make for an impartial and calm judicial consideration and conclusion in the matter."[72]

A 1986 case addressed the propriety of relatives being involved in a quasi-judicial matter. In this case, Leiphart v. North Carolina School of the Arts,[73] a dismissed teacher contended that there was impermissible bias because the daughter of the state personnel director had served as attorney for the school in the appeal of the dismissal to the State Personnel Commission. The Court of Appeals noted that the state bar had ruled that the daughter should not participate in these matters in the future because her participation presented an unacceptable appearance of impropriety. However, the dismissal of the teacher was allowed to stand because there was no showing that the father had in any way participated in the decision or that the daughter's participation had resulted in the hearing officer's or the commission's having the kind of personal stake in the decision that would have created a disqualifying bias.

---

71. 193 N.C. 304, 136 S.E. 868 (1927). In other cases, principally involving clerks and notaries public, the court has ruled that being a relative of a party is not disqualifying absent some other pecuniary interest by the official involved [McAllister v. Purcell, 124 N.C. 262, 32 S.E. 715 (1899) (law does not invalidate acknowledgment taken before officer who has no interest in matter and is not party simply because he is related to parties; although "propriety might discourage" this, it is not illegal); Holmes v. Carr, 163 N.C. 122, 79 S.E. 413 (1913); Branch Investment Co. v. Wooten, 198 N.C. 452, 152 S.E. 167 (1930)].

72. 233 N.C. 699, 704, 65 S.E.2d 356, 359 (1951). The court quoted Burns in stating the essence of the case: "'If self the wavering balance shake, / It's rarely right adjusted'" ("Epistle to a Young Friend") [*Id.* at 703].

73. 80 N.C. App. 339, 342 S.E.2d 914, *review denied*, 318 N.C. 507, 349 S.E.2d 862 (1986).

In another case involving disqualification based on prior personal association with the parties, the court ruled in NCNB Bank v. Gillespie[74] that a judge should have referred a recusal motion to another judge when the defendant asked that the judge be removed on the basis of (1) the defendant family's prior "unfriendly termination" of an attorney-client relationship with the judge; (2) the judge's prior prosecution of the defendant on a previous, unrelated criminal charge; and (3) the judge's business and personal dealings with the plaintiff bank and its employees.

---

74. 291 N.C. 303, 230 S.E.2d 375 (1976).

CHAPTER FIVE

Conclusions

Governmental land-use decisions have a profound effect on communities and individuals. Through such decisions the quality and the character of the state's future development are in large part determined. The decisions also can significantly affect individual landowners' rights. It is therefore imperative that they be made fairly and impartially. Given that many of them are made by citizen officials selected in part because of knowledge and active experience in land-use matters, maintaining impartiality and avoiding conflicts of interest can be difficult.

Financial Conflicts of Interest

State law requires that those entrusted with governmental land-use decision-making authority avoid financial conflicts of interest. This requirement applies to elected and appointed officials at both the state and the local level. It encompasses any participation that is likely to affect the outcome of the decision, not just voting.

Application of the policy against financial conflicts of interest to legislative land-use decisions is particularly difficult. Representatives of various public interest groups serve on public boards. It is expected that they will use their knowledge and experience to advance their groups' interests and that the greater public good will be served by the open debate and compromise that results from such deliberations. Yet although vigorous advocacy of an ideology or a personal perspective is acceptable, using a public office to secure private gain is not. In some instances what is consistent with the ideological views of the member is also good for his or her personal finances. However, such an apparent conflict of interest, even if it has not actually motivated the member's vote, undermines the public confidence in the fairness and the impartiality of the board's decision. Therefore, if a particular legislative land-use decision has the potential to affect a citizen board member's interest in a substantial way, the board member should not participate in that decision.

This conclusion raises the difficult question of determining how substantial the member's financial interest must be to warrant nonparticipation.[1] With many legislative land-use decisions the action taken will have at least a modest impact on all who vote because they are all residents of the community being regulated. The likelihood of personal interest affecting the decision, though, at least in terms of public perceptions and confidence, is directly related to the extent of the member's financial interest.

Therefore with legislative land-use decisions nonparticipation should be required only when the decision has the potential to affect the board member's financial condition in a specific, substantial, and readily identifiable way (as opposed to a remote or speculative way).[2] For advisory decisions the law may not absolutely mandate nonparticipation, but full disclosure of the interest is warranted, and nonparticipation is advisable. With quasi-judicial decisions even the appearance of a conflict of interest must be avoided, so a relatively small or indirect financial interest warrants recusal.

Nonfinancial Conflicts of Interest

Nonfinancial conflicts and bias also must be eliminated in quasi-judicial decisions. Personal bias, predisposition on the merits of the matter, or close personal association with any of the parties disqualifies a member from any involvement with the decision.[3] For example, if a member has taken a prior position on a matter subsequently coming before the board for a quasi-judicial hearing,

---

1. It should be noted that *financial interest* is a more encompassing term than *employment*.

2. For example, the State Board of Ethics on January 22, 1988, advised a Duke Power Co. employee who was a citizen board member that participation in any matter that would be of specific benefit to Duke Power was not acceptable, but participation in matters generally affecting all generators of low-level radioactive waste was acceptable.

3. Although prior expressions of opinion and a strong ideological orientation may well be acceptable for legislative land-use decisions, they may on occasion raise concerns with quasi-judicial decisions. Because these decisions are not making new law but are restricted to an application of existing law to a particular set of facts, a member must be careful not to allow his or her personal feelings or policy orientation to diminish the impartiality of the judgment.

the member should carefully consider whether he or she can honestly approach the matter with an open mind. If the member already has a fixed opinion, he or she should disqualify himself or herself.

Nonparticipation

Once it is determined that a member has a conflict of interest, a question arises as to just how complete his or her nonparticipation in consideration of the matter must be. Does nonparticipation simply mean not voting, or does it also preclude participating in the debate on the matter? May the member temporarily step down from the board and address the remaining members as a citizen? In the absence of statutory guidance, courts in other states have split on this question.[4]

Because any involvement by a member with a conflict of interest tends to undermine public confidence in the board's decision, nonparticipation should extend beyond abstaining from voting to preclude any active involvement in the board's consideration of that matter. Many ethics codes specifically prohibit

---

4. *See* cases cited in ch. 3, notes 9–21.

Courts addressing this question have split on the extent of nonparticipation required. In Hayden v. City of Port Townsend, 28 Wash. App. 192, 622 P.2d 1291 (1981), and Netluch v. Mayor and Council of Borough of West Patterson, 130 N.J. Super. 104, 325 A.2d 517 (1974), courts ruled that participation in discussion without voting was impermissible in situations in which recusal was required. In Bove v. Bd. of Review, 95 R.I. 197, 185 A.2d 751 (1962), the Rhode Island court ruled that it would be improper for a member to chair a hearing (though the member was not voting) in a matter in which recusal was required. The Georgia court in Dunaway v. Marietta, 251 Ga. 727, 308 S.E.2d 823 (1983), ruled that when the vice-president of an applicant corporation chaired one of two planning commission hearings on a matter but did not vote, a factual issue of potential fraud and corruption was presented that should be submitted to a jury.

The Rhode Island court sanctioned, absent any other evidence of undue influence, the testimony before a board of a fellow board member who was disqualified for that individual matter [Tramonti v. Zoning Bd. of Review, 93 R.I. 131, 172 A.2d 93 (1961)]. In this case the disqualified board member was an abutting-property owner testifying in favor of granting a special exception for a multifamily housing project. An alternate had taken his place on the board for this matter. Also a Wisconsin decision upheld a governing board zoning amendment when a member with a conflict participated in the meeting but abstained from voting [Ballenger v. Door County, 131 Wis. 2d 422, 388 N.W.2d 624 (1986)]. *See also In re* Appeal of Stagebrush Promotions, Inc., 98 Pa. Commw. 634, 512 A.2d 776, *appeal denied*, 514 Pa. 637, 522 A.2d 1106 (1986), in which the court ruled that it was not impermissible bias for a member with prejudgment to announce his opposition and recusal and then remain present for the rest of the meeting.

One court has ruled that when the circumstances that led to recusal are removed, the board member may revoke his or her recusal [Morrison v. Dist. of Columbia Bd. of Zoning Adjustment, 422 A.2d 347 (1980)].

attempts by a member with a conflict to influence a decision. This bars discussing, testifying, or even informally advocating an outcome. The North Carolina state bar has published an ethics opinion for attorneys who serve on governing boards that is instructive in this regard. The ruling prohibits members from hearing or considering any matter coming before the board in which the member (or the member's law firm) has a direct or indirect interest. In such situations

> that member shall: (1) disclose in writing or in open meeting to that governing board or entity his relationship to the matter involved, (2) refrain from any expression of opinion, public or private, on, or any formal or informal consideration of, the matter involved, including any communication or other form of contact with other members or staff of the governing body or entity concerning that matter, (3) absent himself from all meetings of the governing body or entity during any discussion or hearing of the matter, (4) withdraw from all voting on the matter, with or without the consent of the governing body or entity.[5]

Absent such a statutory or ordinance provision, under North Carolina law, participation in legislative and advisory decisions as a witness or a citizen is inadvisable, but probably not illegal. However, in quasi-judicial matters, to ensure a completely unbiased decision, members with a conflict of interest must not participate in any manner.

Remedies

If a citizen board member fails to follow these requirements, the courts may well invalidate the action taken and send the matter back to the board for a properly conducted reconsideration.[6] This is costly and time-consuming for the government, the applicant, and the person challenging the action and can be avoided by careful consideration of conflict-of-interest standards at the outset. Also, in some circumstances the member who participates in spite of having a

---

5. Ethics Committee, N.C. State Bar, Revised CPR 290 (October 14, 1981). The rules of the North Carolina House of Representatives also address this question, prohibiting members who have been excused from voting on a matter from participation in other action on the matter: "The member so excused shall not debate the bill or any amendment to the bill, vote on the bill, offer or vote on any amendment to the bill, or offer or vote on any motion concerning the bill at that reading, any subsequent reading, or any subsequent consideration of the bill" [Rule 24.1A, N.C. House of Representatives, 1989 General Assembly (adopted Jan. 11, 1989)].

6. *See, e.g.*, Thorne v. Zoning Comm'rs of Town of Old Saybrook, 178 Conn. 198, 423 A.2d 861 (1979); Smith v. City of Shelbyville, 462 N.E.2d 1052 (Ind. App. 1st Dist. 1984); Hallenborg v. Town Clerk of Billerica, 360 Mass. 513, 275 N.E.2d 525 (1971); Deal Gardens, Inc. v. Bd. of Trustees, 48 N.J. 492, 226 A.2d 607 (1967).

conflict of interest may be subject to individual sanctions, such as censure, removal from office, or even criminal prosecution,[7] and the board involved may be subject to payment of monetary damages.

Written Code

Given the complexity of this question and the possibilities for misunderstandings, citizen boards charged with land-use decision making should give serious consideration to adopting a written code on conflicts of interest. Adoption of such a code in advance of a conflict-of-interest controversy has several advantages. It allows board members and others to give rational and considered thought to this complex matter rather than their having to react to what frequently are emotionally charged individual controversies allowing little time for thoughtful deliberation. It also serves an educational purpose in letting decision makers, landowners, interest groups, and citizens explore the issue and set clear ground rules and expectations before conflicts arise. Although avoiding conflicts of interest requires self-policing and depends to a large degree on the personal integrity of those involved in land-use decision making, ethics guidelines can assist public bodies and the citizens who serve on them in meeting their obligation to provide a fair and unbiased decision-making process.

Some contend that ethics must be self-policing and cannot be mandated by codes. During the debate over adoption of a comprehensive federal conflict-of-interest statute in the early 1960s, well-known New York municipal official Robert Moses contended, "What we need is better men, not more laws to guarantee their competence and honesty."[8] Others express concern that any code, even one stressing that it is setting minimum standards of ethical conduct, in effect becomes the maximum standard required, and any act not specifically prohibited is considered legally and morally acceptable.

---

7.   The Greensboro code provides that a member may be removed from office if the city's financial conflict-of-interest policy is violated [Greensboro Code § 2-142]. Similarly the General Assembly's Legislative Ethics Act provides that either house may censure, suspend, or expel any member whom it finds guilty of unethical conduct [G.S. 120-103(d)(3)].

A Texas court upheld such a removal provision in the face of various constitutional challenges [Price v. City of San Marcos, 744 S.W.2d 349 (Tex. Ct. App. 1988), *cert. denied*, 109 S. Ct. 485 (1988)]. The ordinance involved prohibited all city officials from appearing before any city commission or board; a planning commission member was removed from office after he appeared before the zoning board to request a variance from parking requirements for his wife's business.

8.   Moses, *Mr. Moses Examines Conflict of Interest*, N. Y. Times, July 23, 1961, § 6 (Magazine) at 13.

It is true that a "good" code may not prevent improper actions by a "bad" citizen board member, as it is also true that a "good" board member does not need a code to mandate acceptable behavior. The conclusion of this book is that it is possible and desirable to have both "good" citizen board members and a "good" ethics code. As one commentator concluded:

> Statutory prohibitions alone will not suffice to prevent the occurrence or suspicion of the [conflict of interest] problem. Government officials must acquire true dedication to the concept that "public office is a public trust." Yet it is equally clear that situations can and do arise which require some sort of standard to determine their consistency with the public trust. The greatest usefulness of conflicts of interest legislation is in the provision of these standards.[9]

Care must be exercised in developing a code to make requirements clear and simple to follow.[10] The code should have lofty aspirations, but be capable of realistic implementation. As succinctly put by a former president of the Federal Bar Association, in drafting a conflict-of-interest code, one must "walk a line between a rigid requirement that a monastic oath be taken to relinquish all worldly goods and one in which the candidate is given a secular grant to hunt without a license on the government's preserves."[11] A conflict-of-interest code should set forth general policies on conflicts of interest, desired financial disclosure requirements, and the circumstances under which the board expects its members to disqualify themselves.[12]

A written conflict-of-interest code also allows a clear procedure to be established for deciding who determines whether a conflict exists. A means of securing competent and timely legal advice on a question is a useful part of a code of ethics. Such an independent evaluation relieves the board member with the potential conflict of the decision of whether a conflict exists, a decision that is not

---

9. Eisenberg, *Conflicts of Interest Situations and Remedies*, 13 RUTGERS L. REV. 666, 700 (1959).

10. As commentators noted almost forty years ago, before the imposition of most current ethics requirements, "There is a danger that in attempting to legislate morals we are likely to surround the Government service with so many snares, snags and spring-guns that only the unwary can be recruited" [McElwain and Vorenberg, *The Federal Conflict of Interest Statutes*, 65 HARV. L. REV. 955, 955 (1952)].

11. Philos, Foreword to *Conflicts of Interest—A Symposium*, 24 FED. B.J. 233 (1964).

12. With city councils and boards of county commissioners, this would contain guidelines on when members would request the board to vote to excuse them from participation, because these elected officials may not excuse themselves from voting. The Legislative Ethics Act also requires legislators to disqualify themselves if a conflict of interest would "impair [their] independence of judgment" [G.S. 120-88].

likely to instill public confidence if made by the board member alone. Judges are not required to pass on motions to recuse themselves, and neither should citizen board members be. The Charlotte code provides that a city official may seek an advisory opinion from the city attorney if he or she has doubts as to the applicability of the ethics code. State citizen board members may seek opinions from the State Board of Ethics. Legislators may seek advisory opinions from the Legislative Ethics Committee. Including a provision in local ethics codes allowing board members to refer close calls on participation to an outside party such as the city or county attorney should be carefully considered.

A model conflict-of-interest ordinance is set out in Appendix A.[13] It includes all three approaches that have been used to address this issue—a general aspirational statement of policy, financial disclosure requirements, and regulations to prohibit specific types of conflicts of interest—along with the needed administrative provisions. Such an ordinance can be adopted, in whole or in part, by a city or county governing board and applied to any or all of its appointed citizen boards, councils, and commissions. Also, appointed boards, including state commissions, can adapt these provisions for adoption as part of their own bylaws or internal operating procedures.

North Carolina is fortunate in having thousands of dedicated citizens volunteering to serve their state and local governments in land-use matters. Conflict of interest is just one part of the larger issue of ethics in government, but it is a key element in maintaining broad public confidence in land-use decisions. Ensuring a public perception that the process is fair and that decisions are made with integrity warrants the careful and continuing attention of all involved in land-use decision making.

---

13. For a broader model ethics code applicable to staff and officials, see Freilich and Larson, *Conflicts of Interest: A Model Statutory Proposal for the Regulation of Municipal Transactions,* 38 UMKC L. REV. 373 (1970). For a proposed code regarding conflicts between local government bodies with differing missions, see Larson, *A Model Ethical Code for Appointed Municipal Officials,* 9 HAMLINE J. OF PUB. L. & POL'Y 395 (1989).

Model Ordinance on Conflicts of Interest

Model Ordinance on Conflicts of Interest

SECTION —. CONFLICTS OF INTEREST

1. Purpose

Service on a board, a council, or a commission of the [city/county] of [name] is a public trust. Members of governmental boards have a duty to represent the public interest fairly and honestly. To protect the integrity of governmental decisions and to promote public confidence in the decisions, no board member shall use his or her position for private gain. Further, board members shall refrain from actions that might reasonably call into question the impartiality and the fairness of those decisions. To that end this section establishes minimum standards that board members shall follow to avoid conflicts of interest in governmental decision making. It is the intention of the governing board that this ordinance be liberally construed so as to accomplish its purpose of protecting the public against governmental decisions affected by undue conflicts of interest.

2. Applicability

a. This section shall apply to the citizen members of all "boards" of the [city/county] of [name]. For purposes of this section "boards" includes the [city council/board of commissioners, board of adjustment, planning board, housing authority, redevelopment authority, (list all desired)].

b. This section shall apply to all board members serving on or after [date].

3. Financial Disclosure Statements

a.   Within thirty days of taking office, members of all boards shall file with the [city/county] clerk a financial disclosure statement that complies with this section.

b.   The financial disclosure statement required by this section shall be filed on a form provided by the [city/county] clerk. The clerk shall provide a copy of the form and a copy of this section to each board member affected no less than twenty days before its due date.

c.   The financial disclosure statement shall include the following information:

1.   A listing of all real estate holdings (including legal, equitable, beneficial, and contractual interests) in the [city/county], including any extraterritorial jurisdiction, owned in whole or in part by the member or a member of his or her household;

2.   A listing of all businesses, firms, corporations, and/or partnerships, of whatever nature, operating within the [city/county] for which the member or a member of his or her household has either a 10 percent or greater ownership interest or an ownership interest valued at $5,000 or more; and

3.   A listing of all employers and employees from which or to which the member or a member of his or her household paid or received pay of $5,000 or more in the previous year.

d.   By January 30 of each year the member shall file an updated financial disclosure statement.

e.   The [city/county] clerk shall maintain copies of all required financial statements available for public inspection during regular business hours.

4. Participation in Decisions Affecting Personal Interests

a.   In order to preserve public confidence in the integrity of the governmental process, it shall be the duty of the member of every board covered by this section to avoid even the appearance of conflict of interest. Therefore no such member shall vote on, discuss, debate, advocate, influence, or otherwise participate before the board on which he or she is a member in any matter that would substantially affect, directly or indirectly, his or her personal financial interests or the financial interests of a member of his or her household.[1] This prohibition

---

1.   Unless enabling legislation is secured, several of the provisions of this model ordinance may need to be amended if applied to governing boards. These include Section 4(a) to the extent that it applies to the financial interests of people other than the member directly; Section 6(c) to the extent that it bars the member from voting on the

includes formal and informal consideration of the matter by the board, whether conducted in public or in private.

b.   This provision does not prohibit participation in legislative and advisory decisions that will have a similar effect on all citizens of [city/county name] or in which the financial interest is so insignificant or remote that it is unlikely to affect the member's official actions in any way.

5. Quasi-Judicial Decisions

a.   Members of boards making quasi-judicial decisions shall disqualify themselves from any matter in which their impartiality might reasonably be questioned. Members shall therefore refrain from all participation in any matter in which they have any financial interest (direct or indirect), a personal bias or prejudice, or a personal or financial relationship with any of the parties or the parties' representatives.

b.   In order to ensure a fair and unbiased hearing on the record of all quasi-judicial matters, board members making quasi-judicial decisions shall refrain from discussion of such matters with the parties thereto other than through the formal hearing process.

6. Legal Opinions and Disqualification

a.   Any official covered by this section may seek an opinion from the [city/county] attorney as to the applicability of this section to a particular decision or set of facts. The response to such a request shall be made to the member making the request, and a copy shall be provided to the chair of the body to which the member belongs.

b.   By majority vote, any [city/county] board may seek the opinion of the [city/county] attorney as to the applicability of this section to a particular decision or set of facts.

c.   If an opinion is received from the [city/county] attorney that a member has an impermissible conflict of interest pursuant to this section and the member does not recuse himself or herself, the board may by majority vote (not considering the vote of the member with the alleged conflict) disqualify that member from all participation in the matter involved.[1]

7. Enforcement

a.   If a member participates in a decision in violation of this section, the decision of the board shall be void, and the matter shall be reheard without that member's participation. If no objection to the member's participation has been

---

disqualification question; and Section 7(c) regarding forfeiture of membership upon conviction of a violation of this ordinance.

filed with the board making the decision within ten days of the decision, this section shall be deemed to have been complied with.

b. Any member who fails to make a timely filing of the financial disclosure statement required by this section or intentionally participates in a decision for which this section requires disqualification shall be guilty of a misdemeanor and shall be subject to such penalties as provided by G.S. 14-4.

c. Upon conviction of such offense the member shall forfeit his or her seat on the board, and the member's seat on the board shall be considered vacant as of the date of the final judgment of conviction.[1]

Key Statutes, Codes, and Other Legal Provisions

Key Statutes, Codes, and Other Legal Provisions

1. Statutes

14-234
15A-1223
18B-201
120-85 to -106
150B-32(b), (c), -40
153A-43, -44
160A-74, -75

2. Executive Order

Executive Order No. 1
January 31, 1985
Governor James G. Martin

3. Code of Judicial Conduct

Canons 3(A), (C), (D)

4. Local Codes

City of Charlotte Code
Town of Chapel Hill
    Charter
City of Greensboro Code
    of Ordinances
Guilford County Code
Orange County Code

Statutes

§ 14-234. Director of public trust contracting for his own benefit; participation in business transaction involving public funds; exemptions.

(a) If any person appointed or elected a commissioner or director to discharge any trust wherein the State or any county, city or town may be in any manner interested shall become an undertaker, or make any contract for his own benefit, under such authority, or be in any manner concerned or interested in making such contract, or in the profits thereof, either privately or openly, singly or jointly with another, he shall be guilty of a misdemeanor. Provided, that this section shall not apply to public officials transacting business with banks or banking institutions or savings and loan associations or public utilities regulated under the provisions of Chapter 62 of the General Statutes in regular course of business: Provided further, that such undertaking or contracting shall be authorized by said governing board by specific resolution on which such public official shall not vote.

(b) Nothing in this section nor in any general principle of common law shall render unlawful the acceptance of remuneration from a governmental board, agency or commission for services, facilities, or supplies furnished directly to needy individuals by a member of said board, agency or commission under any program of direct public assistance being rendered under the laws of this State or the United States to needy persons administered in whole or in part by such board, agency or commission; provided, however, that such programs of public assistance to needy persons are open to general participation on a nondiscriminatory basis to the practitioners of any given profession, professions or occupation; and provided further that the board, agency or commission, nor any of its employees or agents, shall have no control over who, among licensed or qualified providers, shall be selected by the beneficiaries of the assistance, and that the remuneration for such services, facilities or supplies shall be in the same amount as would be paid to any other provider; and provided further that, although the board, agency or commission member may participate in making determinations of eligibility of needy persons to receive the assistance, he shall take no part in approving his own bill or claim for remuneration.

(c) No director, board member, commissioner, or employee of any State department, agency, or institution shall directly or indirectly enter into or otherwise participate in any business transaction involving public funds with any firm, corporation, partnership, person or association which at any time during the preceding two-year period had a financial association with such director, board member, commissioner or employee.

(c1) The fact that a person owns ten percent (10%) or less of the stock of a corporation or has a ten percent (10%) or less ownership in any other business entity or is an employee of said corporation or other business entity does not make the person "in any manner interested" or "concerned or interested in making such contract, or in the profits thereof," as such phrase is used in subsection (a) of this section, and does not make the person one who "had a financial association," as defined in subsection (c) of this section; provided that in order for the exception provided by this subsection to apply, such undertaking or contracting must be authorized by the governing board by specific resolution on which such public official shall not vote.

(d) The provisions of subsection (c) shall not apply to any trans-actions meeting the requirements of Article 3, Chapter 143 of the General Statutes or any other transaction specifically authorized by the Advisory Budget Commission.

(d1) The first sentence of subsection (a) shall not apply to (i) any elected official or person appointed to fill an elective office of a village, town, or city having a population of no more than 7,500 according to the most recent official federal census, (ii) any elected official or person appointed to fill an elective office of a county within which there is located no village, town, or city with a population of more than 7,500 according to the most recent official federal census, (iii) any elected official or person appointed to fill an elective office on a city board of education in a city having a population of no more than 7,500 according to the most recent official federal census, (iv) any elected official or person appointed to fill an elective office as a member of a county board of education in a county within which there is located no village, town or city with a population of more than 7,500 according to the most recent official federal census, (v) any physician, pharmacist, dentist, optometrist, veterinarian, or nurse appointed to a county social services board, local health board, or area mental health board serving one or more counties within which there is located no village, town, or city with a population of more than 7,500 according to the most recent official federal census, and (vi) any member of the board of directors of a public hospital if:

    (1) The undertaking or contract or series of undertakings or contracts between the village, town, city, county, county social services board, county or city board of education, local health board or area mental health, mental retardation, and substance abuse board, or public hospital and one of its officials is approved by specific resolution of the governing body adopted in an open and public meeting, and recorded in its minutes and the amount does not exceed ten thousand dollars ($10,000) for medically related

services and fifteen thousand dollars ($15,000) for other goods or services within a 12-month period; and

(2) The official entering into the contract or undertaking with the unit or agency does not in his official capacity participate in any way or vote; and

(3) The total annual amount of undertakings or contracts with each official, shall be specifically noted in the audited annual financial statement of the village, town, city, or county; and

(4) The governing board of any village, town, city, county, county social services board, county or city board of education, local health board, area mental health, mental retardation, and substance abuse board, or public hospital which undertakes or contracts with any of the officials of their governmental unit shall post in a conspicuous place in its village, town, or city hall, or courthouse, as the case may be, a list of all such officials with whom such undertakings or contracts have been made, briefly describing the subject matter of the undertakings or contracts and showing their total amounts; this list shall cover the preceding 12 months and shall be brought up-to-date at least quarterly.

(d2) The provision of subsection (d1) shall not apply to contracts required by Article 8 of Chapter 143 of the General Statutes, Public Building Contracts.

(e) Anyone violating this section shall be guilty of a misdemeanor.

§ 15A-1223. Disqualification of judge.

(a) A judge on his own motion may disqualify himself from presiding over a criminal trial or other criminal proceeding.

(b) A judge, on motion of the State or the defendant, must disqualify himself from presiding over a criminal trial or other criminal proceeding if he is:

(1) Prejudiced against the moving party or in favor of the adverse party; or

(2) Repealed.

(3) Closely related to the defendant by blood or marriage; or

(4) For any other reason unable to perform the duties required of him in an impartial manner.

(c) A motion to disqualify must be in writing and must be accompanied by one or more affidavits setting forth facts relied upon to show the grounds for disqualification.

(d) A motion to disqualify a judge must be filed no less than five days before the time the case is called for trial unless good cause is shown for failure to file within that time. Good cause includes the discovery of facts constituting grounds for disqualification less than five days before the case is called for trial.

(e) A judge must disqualify himself from presiding over a criminal trial or proceeding if he is a witness for or against one of the parties in the case.

§ 18B-201. Conflict of interest.

(a) Financial Interests Restricted.—No person shall be appointed to or employed by the Commission, a local board, or the ALE Division, if that person or a member of his household related to him by blood or marriage has or controls, directly or indirectly, a financial interest in any commercial alcoholic beverage enterprise, including any business required to have an ABC permit. The Commission may exempt from this provision any person, other than a Commission member, when the financial interest in question is so insignificant or remote that it is unlikely to affect the person's official actions in any way. Exemptions may be granted only to individuals, not to groups or classes of people, and each exemption shall be in writing, be available for public inspection, and contain a statement of the financial interest in question.

(b) Self-dealing.—The provisions of G.S. 14-234 shall apply to the Commission and local boards.

(c) Dealing for Family Members.—Neither the Commission nor any local board shall contract or otherwise deal in any business matter so that a member's spouse or any person related to him by blood to a degree of first cousin or closer in any way benefits, directly or indirectly, from the transaction unless:

(1) The member whose relative benefits from the transaction abstains from participating in any way, including voting, in the decision;

(2) The minutes of the meeting at which the final decision is reached specifically note the member whose spouse or relative is benefited and the amount involved in each transaction;

(3) The next annual audit of the Commission or local board specifically notes the member and the amount involved in each transaction occurring during the year covered by the audit; and

(4) If the transaction is by a local board, the Commission is notified at least two weeks before final board approval of the transaction.

§ 120-85. Definitions.

As used in this Article:

(1) "Business with which he is associated" means any enterprise, incorporated or otherwise, doing business in the State of which the

legislator or any member of his immediate household is a director, officer, owner, partner, employee, or of which the legislator and his immediate household, either singularly or collectively, is a holder of securities worth five thousand dollars ($5,000) or more at fair market value as of December 31 of the preceding year, or constituting five percent (5%) or more of the outstanding stock of such enterprise.

(2) "Immediate household" means the legislator, his spouse, and all dependent children of the legislator.

(3) "Vested trust" as set forth in G.S. 120-96(4) means any trust, annuity or other funds held by a trustee or other third party for the benefit of the member or a member of his immediate household.

§ 120-86. Bribery, etc.

(a) No person shall offer or give to a legislator or a member of a legislator's immediate household, or to a business with which he is associated, and no legislator shall solicit or receive, anything of monetary value, including a gift, favor or service or a promise of future employment, based on any understanding that such legislator's vote, official actions or judgment would be influenced thereby, or where it could reasonably be inferred that the thing of value would influence the legislator in the discharge of his duties.

(b) It shall be unlawful for the partner, client, customer, or employer of a legislator or the agent of that partner, client, customer, or employer to threaten economically, directly or indirectly, that legislator with the intent to influence the legislator in the discharge of his legislative duties.

(c) It shall be unethical for a legislator to contact the partner, client, customer, or employer of another legislator if the purpose of the contact is to cause the partner, client, customer, or employer to threaten economically, directly or indirectly, that legislator with the intent to influence that legislator in the discharge of his legislative duties.

(d) For the purposes of this section, the term "legislator" also includes any person who has been elected or appointed to the General Assembly but who has not yet taken the oath of office.

(e) Violation of subsection (a) or (b) is a Class I felony. Violation of subsection (c) is not a crime but is punishable under G.S. 120-103.

§ 120-87. Disclosure of confidential information.

No legislator shall use or disclose confidential information gained in the course of or by reason of his official position or activities in any way that could result in financial gain for himself, a business with which he is associated or a member of his immediate household or any other person.

§ 120-88. When legislator to disqualify himself or submit question to Legislative Ethics Committee.

When a legislator must act on a legislative matter as to which he has an economic interest, personal, family, or client, he shall consider whether his judgment will be substantially influenced by the interest, and consider the need for his particular contribution, such as special knowledge of the subject matter, to the effective functioning of the legislature. If after considering these factors the legislator concludes that an actual economic interest does exist which would impair his independence of judgment, then he shall not take any action to further the economic interest, and shall ask that he be excused, if necessary, by the presiding officer in accordance with the rules of the respective body. If the legislator has a material doubt as to whether he should act, he may submit the question to the Legislative Ethics Committee for an advisory opinion in accordance with G.S. 120-104.

§ 120-89. Statement of economic interest by legislative candidates; filing required.

Every person who files as a candidate for nomination or election to a seat in either house of the General Assembly shall file a statement of economic interest as specified in this Article within 10 days of the filing deadline for the office he seeks.

§ 120-90. Place and manner of filing.

The statement of economic interest shall cover the preceding calendar year and shall be filed at the same place, and in the same manner, as the notice of candidacy which a candidate seeking party nomination for the office of State Senator or member of the State House of Representatives is required to file under the provisions of G.S. 163-106.

§ 120-91. Repealed.

§ 120-92. Filing by candidates not nominated in primary elections.

A person who is nominated pursuant to the provisions of G.S. 163-114 after the primary and before the general election, and a person who qualifies pursuant to the provisions of G.S. 163-122 as an independent candidate in a general election shall file with the county board of elections of each county in the senatorial or representative district a statement of economic interest. A person nominated pursuant to G.S. 163-114 shall file the statement within three days following his nomination, or not later than the day preceding the general election, whichever occurs first. A person seeking to qualify as an independent candidate under G.S. 163-122 shall file the statement of economic interest with the petition filed pursuant to that section.

§ 120-93. County boards of elections to notify candidates of economic-interest-statement requirements.

Each county board of elections shall provide for notification of the economic-interest-statement requirements of G.S. 120-89, 120-96, and 120-98 to be given to any candidate filing for nomination or election to the General Assembly at the time of his or her filing in the particular county.

§ 120-93.1 Certification of statements of economic interest.

The chairman of the county board of elections with which a statement of economic interest is filed shall forward a certified copy of the statement to the Legislative Services Office once the candidate is certified as elected to the General Assembly. The chairman shall also forward a certified copy of each candidate's statement of economic interest, within 10 days after its filing, to the board of elections in each other county in the district the candidate seeks to represent.

§ 120-94. Statements of economic interest are public records.

The statements of economic interest are public records and shall be made available for inspection and copying by any person during normal business hours at the office of the various county boards of election where the statements or copies thereof are filed and at the Legislative Library after certified copies are forwarded to the Legislative Services Office. If a county board of elections of a county does not keep an office open during normal business hours each day, that board shall deliver a copy of all statements of economic interest filed with it to the clerk of superior court of the county, and the statements shall be available for inspection and copying by any person during normal business hours at that clerk's office.

§ 120-95. Repealed.

§ 120-96. Contents of statement.

Any statement of economic interest filed under this Article shall be on a form prescribed by the Committee, and the person filing the statement shall supply the following information:

    (1) The identity, by name, of any business with which he, or any member of his immediate household, is associated;

    (2) The character and location of all real estate of a fair market value

in excess of five thousand dollars ($5,000), other than his personal residence (curtilage), in the State in which he, or a member of his immediate household, has any beneficial interest, including an option to buy and a lease for 10 years or over;

(3) The type of each creditor to whom he, or a member of his immediate household, owes money, except indebtedness secured by lien upon his personal residence only, in excess of five thousand dollars ($5,000);

(4) The name of each "vested trust" in which he or a member of his immediate household has a financial interest in excess of five thousand dollars ($5,000) and the nature of such interest;

(5) The name and nature of his and his immediate household member's respective business or profession or employer and the types of customers and types of clientele served;

(6) A list of businesses with which he is associated that do business with the State, and a brief description of the nature of such business;

(7) In the case of professional persons and associations, a list of classifications of business clients which classes were charged or paid two thousand five hundred dollars ($2,500) or more during the previous calendar year for professional services rendered by him, his firm or partnership. This list need not include the name of the client but shall list the type of the business of each such client or class of client, and brief description of the nature of the services rendered.

§ 120-97. Repealed.

§ 120-98. Penalty for failure to file.

(a) If a candidate does not file the statement of economic interest within the time required by this Article, the county board of elections shall immediately notify the candidate by registered mail, restricted delivery to addressee only, that, if the statement is not received within 15 days, the candidate shall not be certified as the nominee of his party. If the statement is not received within 15 days of notification, the board of elections authorized to certify a candidate as nominee to the office shall not certify the candidate as nominee under any circumstances, regardless of the number of candidates for the nomination and regardless of the number of votes the candidate receives in the primary. A vacancy thus created on a party's ticket shall be considered a vacancy for the purposes of G.S. 163-114, and shall be filled according to the procedures set out in G.S. 163-114.

(b) Repealed.

§ 120-99. Creation; composition.

The Legislative Ethics Committee is created to consist of a chairman and eight members, four Senators appointed by the President of the Senate, two from a list of four submitted by the Majority Leader and two from a list of four submitted by the Minority Leader, and four members of the House of Representatives appointed by the Speaker of the House, two from a list of four submitted by the Majority Leader and two from a list of four submitted by the Minority Leader.

The President of the Senate shall designate a member of the General Assembly as chairman of the Committee in odd-numbered years, and the Speaker of the House shall designate a member of the General Assembly as chairman of the Committee in even-numbered years. The chairman will vote only in the event of a tie vote.

The provisions of G.S. 120-19.1 through G.S. 120-19.8 shall apply to the proceedings of the Legislative Ethics Committee as if it were a joint committee of the General Assembly, except that the chairman shall sign all subpoenas on behalf of the Committee.

§ 120-100. Term of office; vacancies.

Initial members of the Legislative Ethics Committee shall be appointed as soon as practicable after the ratification of this Article and shall serve until the expiration of their current terms as members of the General Assembly. Thereafter, appointments shall be made immediately after the convening of the regular session of the General Assembly in odd-numbered years, and appointees shall serve until the expiration of their then-current terms as members of the General Assembly. The chairman shall serve for one year and shall be appointed each year. A vacancy occurring for any reason during a term shall be filled for the unexpired term by the authority making the appointment which caused the vacancy, and the person appointed to fill the vacancy shall, if possible, be a member of the same political party as the member who caused the vacancy.

§ 120-101. Quorum; expenses of members.

Five members constitute a quorum of the Committee. A vacancy on the Committee does not impair the right of the remaining members to exercise all the powers of the Committee.

The chairman and members of the Committee, while serving on the business of the Committee, are performing legislative duties and are entitled to the subsistence and travel allowances to which members of the General Assembly are entitled when performing legislative duties.

§ 120-102. Powers and duties of Committee.

In addition to the other powers and duties specified in this Article, the Committee has the following powers and duties:

(1) To prescribe forms for the statements of economic interest and other reports required by this Article, and to furnish these forms to persons who are required to file statements or reports.

(2) To receive and file any information voluntarily supplied that exceeds the requirements of this Article.

(3) To organize in a reasonable manner statements and reports filed with it and to make these statements and reports available for public inspection and copying during regular office hours. Copying facilities shall be made available at a charge not to exceed actual cost.

(4) To preserve statements and reports filed with the Committee for a period of 10 years from the date of receipt. At the end of the 10-year period, these documents shall be destroyed.

(5) To prepare a list of ethical principles and guidelines to be used by each legislator in determining his role in supporting or opposing specific types of legislation, and to advise each General Assembly committee of specific danger areas where conflict of interest may exist and to suggest rules of conduct that should be adhered to by committee members in order to avoid conflict.

(6) To advise General Assembly committees, at the request of a committee chairman, or at the request of three members of a committee, about possible points of conflict and suggested standards of conduct of committee members in the consideration of specific bills or groups of bills.

(7) To suggest to legislators activities which should be avoided.

(8) Upon receipt of information that a legislator owes money to the State and is delinquent in making repayment of such obligation, to investigate and dispose of the matter according to the terms of this Article.

§ 120-103. Possible violations; procedures; disposition.

(a) Institution of Proceedings.—On its own motion, or in response to signed and sworn complaint of any individual filed with the Committee, the Committee shall inquire into any alleged violation of any provision of this Article.

(b) Notice and Hearing.—If, after such preliminary investigation as it may make, the Committee determines to proceed with an inquiry into the conduct of any individual, the Committee shall notify the individual as to the fact of the inquiry and the charges against him and shall schedule one or more hearings on the matter. The individual shall have the right to present evidence, cross-examine witnesses, and be represented by counsel at any hearings. The Committee may, in its discretion, hold hearings in closed session; however, the individual whose conduct is under inquiry may, by written demand filed with the Committee, require that all hearings before the Committee concerning him be public or in closed session.

(c) Subpoenas.—The Committee may issue subpoenas to compel the attendance of witnesses or the production of documents, books or other records. The Committee may apply to the superior court to compel obedience to the subpoenas of the Committee. Notwithstanding any other provision of law, every State agency, local governmental agency, and units and subdivisions thereof shall make available to the Committee any documents, records, data, statements or other information, except tax returns or information relating thereto, which the Committee designates as being necessary for the exercise of its powers and duties.

(d) Disposition of Cases.— When the Committee has concluded its inquiries into the alleged violations, the Committee may dispose of the matter in one or more of the following ways:

(1) The Committee may dismiss the complaint and take no further action. In such case the Committee shall retain its records and findings in confidence unless the individual under inquiry requests in writing that the records and findings be made public.

(2) The Committee may, if it finds substantial evidence that a criminal statute has been violated, refer the matter to the Attorney General for possible prosecution through appropriate channels.

(3) The Committee may refer the matter to the appropriate House of the General Assembly for appropriate action. That House may, if it finds the member guilty of unethical conduct as defined in this Article, censure, suspend or expel the member.

§ 120-104. Advisory opinions.

At the request of any member of the General Assembly, the Committee shall render advisory opinions on specific questions involving legislative ethics. These advisory opinions, edited as necessary to protect the identity of the legislator requesting the opinion, shall be published periodically by the Committee.

§ 120-105. Continuing study of ethical questions.

The Committee shall conduct continuing studies of questions of legislative ethics including revisions and improvements of this Article as well as sections to cover the administrative branch of government and shall report to the General Assembly from time to time recommendations for amendments to the statutes and legislative rules which the Committee deems desirable in promoting, maintaining and effectuating high standards of ethics in the legislative branch of State government.

§ 120-106. Article applicable to presiding officers.

The provisions of this Article shall apply to the presiding officers of the General Assembly.

§ 150B-32. Designation of administrative law judge.

(b) On the filing in good faith by a party of a timely and sufficient affidavit of personal bias or disqualification of an administrative law judge, the administrative law judge shall determine the matter as a part of the record in the case, and this determination shall be subject to judicial review at the conclusion of the proceeding.

(c) When an administrative law judge is disqualified or it is impracticable for him to continue the hearing, the Director shall assign another administrative law judge to continue with the case unless it is shown that substantial prejudice to any party will result, in which event a new hearing shall be held or the case dismissed without prejudice.

§ 150B-40. Conduct of hearing; presiding officer; ex parte communication.

(a) Hearings shall be conducted in a fair and impartial manner. At the hearing, the agency and the parties shall be given an opportunity to present evidence on issues of fact, examine and cross-examine witnesses, including the author of a document prepared by, on behalf of or for the use of the agency and offered into evidence, submit rebuttal evidence, and present arguments on issues of law or policy.

If a party fails to appear in a contested case after he has been given proper notice, the agency may continue the hearing or proceed with the hearing and make its decision in the absence of the party.

(b) Except as provided under subsection (e) of this section, hearings under this Article shall be conducted by a majority of the agency. An agency shall designate one or more of its members to preside at the hearing. If a party files in good faith a timely and sufficient affidavit of the personal bias or other reason for disqualification of any member of the agency, the agency shall determine the matter as a part of the record in the case, and its determination shall be subject to judicial review at the conclusion of the proceeding. If a presiding officer is disqualified or it is impracticable for him to continue the hearing, another presiding officer shall be assigned to continue with the case, except that if assignment of a new presiding officer will cause substantial prejudice to any party, a new hearing shall be held or the case dismissed without prejudice.

. . . .

(d) Unless required for disposition of an ex parte matter authorized by law, a member of an agency assigned to make a decision or to make findings of fact and conclusions of law in a contested case under this Article shall not communicate, directly or indirectly, in connection with any issue of fact or question of law, with any person or party or his representative, except on notice and opportunity for all parties to participate. This prohibition begins at the time of the notice of hearing. An agency member may communicate with other members of the agency and may have the aid and advice of the agency staff other than the staff which has been or is engaged in investigating or prosecuting functions in connection with the case under consideration or a factually-related case. This section does not apply to an agency employee or party representative with professional training in accounting, actuarial science, economics or financial analysis insofar as the case involves financial practices or conditions.

§ 153A-43. Quorum.

A majority of the membership of the board of commissioners constitutes a quorum. The number required for a quorum is not affected by vacancies. If a member has withdrawn from a meeting without being excused by majority vote of the remaining members present, he shall be counted as present for the purposes of determining whether a quorum is present. The board may compel the attendance of an absent member by ordering the sheriff to take the member into custody.

§ 153A-44. Members excused from voting.

The board may excuse a member from voting, but only upon questions involving his own financial interest or his official conduct. (For purposes of this section, the question of the compensation and allowances of members of the board does not involve a member's own financial interest or official conduct.)

§ 160A-74. Quorum.

A majority of the actual membership of the council plus the mayor, excluding vacant seats, shall constitute a quorum. A member who has withdrawn from a meeting without being excused by majority vote of the remaining members present shall be counted as present for purposes of determining whether or not a quorum is present.

§ 160A-75. Voting.

No member shall be excused from voting except upon matters involving the consideration of his own financial interest or official conduct. In all other cases, a failure to vote by a member who is physically present in the council chamber, or who has withdrawn without being excused by a majority vote of the remaining members present, shall be recorded as an affirmative vote. The question of the compensation and allowances of members of the council is not a matter involving a member's own financial interest or official conduct.

An affirmative vote equal to a majority of all the members of the council not excused from voting on the question in issue (including the mayor's vote in case of an equal division) shall be required to adopt an ordinance, take any action having the effect of an ordinance, authorize or commit the expenditure of public funds, or make, ratify, or authorize any contract on behalf of the city. In addition, no ordinance nor any action having the effect of any ordinance may be finally adopted on the date on which it is introduced except by an affirmative vote equal to or greater than two thirds of all the actual membership of the council, excluding vacant seats (not including the mayor unless he has the right to vote on all questions before the council). For purposes of this section, an ordinance shall be deemed to have been introduced on the date the subject matter is first voted on by the council.

Executive Order

STATE OF NORTH CAROLINA
OFFICE OF THE GOVERNOR
EXECUTIVE ORDER NUMBER 1

January 31, 1985

WHEREAS, public office in North Carolina must always be regarded as a public trust; and

WHEREAS, the people of North Carolina have a fundamental right to the assurance that officers of their government will not use their public position for personal gain; and

WHEREAS, this Administration is committed to restore and maintain the confidence of North Carolina citizens in their government; and

WHEREAS, there is a need in North Carolina for the creation of an institutionalized procedure designed to prevent the occurrence of conflicts of interest in government and to deal with them when they do occur; and

WHEREAS, this Administration realizes that the vast majority of state government employees are honest and hard working in their public and private lives;

NOW, THEREFORE, it is hereby ordered:

Section 1. *Executive Order Number 1, January 10, 1977.*
Executive Order Number 1, dated January 10, 1977, is hereby rescinded. All records, including but not limited to Statements of Economic Interest, of the North Carolina Board of Ethics created pursuant to said executive order, are transferred to the North Carolina Board of Ethics herein.

Section 2. *North Carolina Board of Ethics.* There is hereby established the North Carolina Board of Ethics consisting of five persons to be appointed by the Governor to serve at his pleasure. The Governor shall, from time to time, designate one of the members as Chairman. The members shall receive no compensation, but shall receive reimbursement for any necessary expenses incurred in connection with the performance of their duties pursuant to General Statute 138-15. The Board of Ethics shall not be considered a public office for the purpose of dual office holding.

Section 3. *Persons subject to Order*. The following persons are subject to this order and to the jurisdiction of the Board of Ethics:

(a) All employees in the Office of the Governor.

(b) The heads of all principal departments of state government who are appointed by the Governor.

(c) The chief deputy or chief administrative assistant to each of the aforesaid heads of principal state departments.

(d) All "confidential" assistants or secretaries to the aforesaid department heads (or to the aforesaid chief deputies and assistants of department heads) as defined in G.S. 126-5(b)(2).

(e) All employees in policy-making positions as designated by the Governor pursuant to the State Personnel Act as defined in G.S. 126-5(b)(3), and all "confidential" secretaries to these individuals as defined in G.S. 126-5(b)(4).

(f) Any other employees in the principal departments of state government, except in those principal departments headed by elected heads other than the Governor, as may be designated by rule of the Board subject to the approval of the Governor, to the extent such designation does not conflict with the State Personnel Act.

(g) The members of all commissions, boards and councils appointed by the Governor, with the exception of members of those commissions, boards and councils the Board of Ethics determines perform solely advisory functions.

(h) The elected heads of other principal state departments, and certain employees of those departments as designated by the head, in the event of an election by such department head to participate in the system created by this Order as provided for in Section 8 of this Order.

(i) Members of North Carolina Board of Ethics.

Section 4. *Exemption From Order*. Notwithstanding Section 3, herein, a commission, board or council to which the Governor appoints members, may upon written application request the Board of Ethics to exempt its members from this Order. The Board of Ethics shall make a determination upon such requests, which shall be final, after a specific finding by the Board that such exemption does not violate the intent of this Order [and] in no way interferes or conflicts with the proper and effective discharge of the official duties of the members of the commission, board or council making the request. The determination of the

Board of Ethics in every such case shall be made available for public inspection at a convenient location.

Section 5. *Specific Prohibitions.*
- (a) No person subject to this Order shall engage in any activity which interferes or is in conflict with the proper and effective discharge of such person's official duties.
- (b) No person who is employed by the state in a full-time position and who is subject to this Order, shall hold any other public office or public employment for which compensation, direct or indirect, is received except under circumstances and in the manner approved by the Board upon review of a written request pursuant to Board procedures;
- (c) No person subject to this Order shall solicit in their official capacity [any] gratuity or other benefits for themselves from any other person under any circumstances.

Any exception to the foregoing prohibitions granted by the Board, may only be allowed by the Board upon written application to the Board, and after a specific finding by the Board that such activity does not violate the intent of this Order and in no way interferes or conflicts with the proper and effective discharge of the official duties of the person making the request. The Board shall make a determination in each such case, which shall be final. The determination of the Board in every such case shall be made available for public inspection at a convenient location.

Section 6. *Statements of Economic Interest.*
- (a) Within thirty days from commencement of state service or the effective date of this Order, whichever is later, and thereafter between April 15 and May 15 of each succeeding year, each of the following persons subject to this Order shall file with the Board a sworn Statement of Economic Interest:
  - (i) Each person appointed by the Governor and subject to this Order;
  - (ii) Each person subject to this Order, whether or not appointed by the Governor, who receives $30,000 or more from the state;
  - (iii) Each person subject to this Order, irrespective of the amount of compensation received, whose position is subject to undue influence (as determined from time to time by the Board);

(iv) Each person designated by the elected head of a principal department of state government pursuant to Section 8 of this order;

(v) Statements filed by members of the Board of Ethics shall be filed with the Governor and shall be made public.

(b) The Statement of Economic Interest shall contain:

(i) The name, home address, occupation, employer and business address of the person filing.

(ii) A list of all assets and liabilities of the person filing which exceed a valuation of $5,000. With respect to each asset and liability listed, the specific valuation need not be set forth, but there should be an indication as to whether the valuation of each asset or liability exceeds $10,000. This list shall contain, but shall not be limited to, the following:

(A) All real estate, with specific description adequate to determine the location of each parcel;

(B) The name of each publicly-owned company (companies which are required to register with the Securities and Exchange Commission) in which securities are owned, with an indication as to whether the valuation of the securities owned in each company listed exceeds $10,000.

(C) The name of each non-publicly-owned company or business entity in which securities or other equity interests are owned, and an indication as to whether the valuation of the securities or equity interest owned in each such company or business entity listed exceeds $10,000.

(D) With respect to the aforesaid non-publicly-owned company or business entities in which the interest of the person filing exceeds a valuation of $10,000, if any such companies or business entities own securities or equity interests in other companies or business entities, the name of each such other company or business entity should be listed if the securities or other equity interests in them held by the aforesaid non-publicly-owned company exceed a valuation of $10,000.

(E) If the person filing or his or her spouse or dependent children are the beneficiary of a trust created, established or controlled by the person filing, which holds assets, and if those assets are known, the name of each company or other business entity in which securities or other equity interests are held by the trust should be listed, with an indication as to whether the valuation of the securities or equity interest held in each such company or business entity listed exceed $10,000, and with the name and address of the trustee and a description of the trust. If any of the aforesaid assets are securities or other equity interests in a corporation or other business entity, each such corporation or business entity should be listed separately by name. If the assets [are] held by such a trust [and] the name and address of the trustee should be provided.

(F) A list of all other assets and liabilities which exceed a valuation of $5,000 (including bank accounts and debts), with an indication as to whether each asset and liability exceeds a valuation of $10,000.

(iii) A list of all sources (not specific amounts) of income (including capital gains) shown on the most recent federal and state income tax returns of the person filing where $5,000 or more was received from such source.

(iv) If the person filing is a practicing attorney, check each category of legal representation in which the person filing, and/or his or her law firm has, during any single year of the past five years, earned legal fees in excess of five thousand dollars ($5,000) from any of the following categories of legal representation:

_____ Criminal law
_____ Utilities regulation or representation of regulated utilities
_____ Corporation law
_____ Taxation
_____ Decedent's estates
_____ Insurance law
_____ Administrative law
_____ Real property
_____ Admiralty
_____ Negligence (representing plaintiffs)
_____ Negligence (representing defendants)

(v) A list of all business with which, during the past five years, the person filing has been associated, indicating the time period of such association and the relationship with each business as an officer, employee, director, partner or a material owner of a security or other equity interest and indicating whether or not each does business with or is regulated by the state and the nature of the business, if any, done with state.

(vi) In all statements of economic interest after the first one filed by an individual, a list of all gifts of a value of more than $100 received during the twelve months preceding the date of the Statement of Economic Interest from sources other than relatives of the person filing and his or her spouse, and a list of all gifts, of value of more than $50 received from any source having business with or regulated by the state.

(vii) Other information as may be deemed necessary to effectuate the purpose of this Order, as provided for by rule of the Board.

(viii) A statement setting forth any other information or relationship which the person filing believes may relate to any actual or potential conflict of interest he or she may have as an employee of state government.

(ix) A sworn certification by the person filing that he or she has read the Statement of Economic Interest, and that to the best of his or her knowledge and belief it is true, correct, complete and that he or she has not transferred and will not transfer any asset, interest or other property for the purpose of concealing it from disclosure while retaining an equitable interest therein.

(c) The person filing a Statement of Economic Interest shall list as specified in Section 6(b) the assets, liabilities, and sources of income of his or her spouse which are derived from the assets or income of the person filing, controlled by the person filing, or for which the person filing is jointly or severally liable.

(d) Any person required to file a Statement of Economic Interest or his or her spouse may request the Board to delete an item, which may be deleted by the Board pursuant to a written request, but only upon a finding that it is of a confidential nature, does not in any way relate to the duties of the position held or to be held by such person and does not create an actual or potential conflict of interest.

(e) The Board of Ethics shall issue a form for such Statements of Economic Interest, which in no event shall be later than February 15, 1985.

(f) After review and evaluation by the Board, the Statements of Economic Interest will be made available by the Board for public inspection.

Section 7. *Duties of Board of Ethics.*

(a) The Board shall review all Statements of Economic Interest submitted to it to determine their conformity with the terms of this Order and the Board's rules, and to evaluate the financial interests of the person filing to determine whether there appears to be actual or potential conflicts of interest. The Board shall submit a written report of each such evaluation to the Official responsible for making the appointment of the person filing, and to the Governor, unless the person is an employee of one of the other principal departments of state government listed in Section 8 of this Order, in which case a copy of the written report shall be sent to the elected head of that department. The Board may recommend remedial action with respect to any problem which is apparent from any Statement.

(b) The Board shall evaluate all claims of privacy made concerning a portion of a Statement of Economic Interest, prior to making the Statement available for public inspection, and the decision of the Board in these matters shall be final.

(c) The Board shall provide by rule for the time, place and manner of convenient public inspection of the Statements of Economic Interest.

(d) The Board shall promulgate readily understandable rules, forms and procedures to carry out the purposes of this Order and shall publish them.

(e) The Board shall render opinions and determinations on matters pertaining to the interpretation and application of this Order.

(f) The Board shall provide reasonable assistance to all persons subject to this Order in complying with the terms of this Order.

(g) The Board shall receive information from the public concerning potential conflicts of interest and make necessary investigations. The Board shall promulgate rules to protect all employees from specious and unfounded claims and damage to their reputations which could result from such claims. The Board also shall promulgate rules to protect employees from any direct or indirect reprisals from any source resulting from efforts to inform the Board of the existence of potential or actual conflicts of interest in state government. The Board also shall promulgate rules providing for full and fair consideration of the merits of all complaints received which rules shall assure that the rights of all parties involved in the investigation are protected. All complaints and allegations concerning actual or potential conflicts of interest to be considered by the Board must contain the name, address, telephone number and oath of the individual filing such complaint or making such allegation. The Board shall prepare a report of each such investigation and forward a copy to the official responsible for making the appointment of the person investigated, and to the Governor, unless the person investigated is an employee of one of the other principal departments of state government listed in section 8 of this Order, in which case a copy of the written report shall be sent to the elected head of that department. The Board may recommend remedial action with respect to any problem revealed by such an investigation.

(h) The Board shall request, when necessary to accomplish the purposes of this Order, additional information from persons covered by this Order.

(i) The Board shall meet regularly, at the call of the Chairman, to carry out its duties.

(j) The Board shall submit a report annually to the Governor on their activities and generally on the subject of public disclosure, ethics and conflicts of interest, including recommendations for administrative and legislative action.

(k) The Board shall perform such other duties as may be necessary to accomplish the purposes of this Order.

Section 8. *Other Principal Departments of State Government.* The elected heads of other principal departments of the state government (Office of the Lieutenant Governor, Departments of the Secretary of State, State Auditor, State Treasurer, Public Education, Justice, Agriculture, Labor and Insurance) and the University of North Carolina Board of Governors may, and hereby are invited to, join in the effort represented by this Order by providing the Chairman of the Board of Ethics with a written notice of their election to have the terms of this Order apply to those employees under their jurisdiction (who are not covered by the State Personnel Act), and with a list of the employees under their jurisdiction who will be asked to submit a Statement of Economic Interest. All services of the Board available to the Governor under this Order shall be available to each of the heads of the aforesaid departments so electing, and all of the services of the Board available to employees under this order shall be available to employees brought within the coverage of this Order in this manner.

Section 9. *Sanctions.* The failure [of] any employee to make timely filing of a required document, the making of a false or misleading statement or an omission in a document, the failure to cooperate with the Board of Ethics and the failure to comply with the terms of this Order, shall be grounds for disciplinary action, including discharge.

Section 10. *Board Offices.* The Board of Ethics and its staff, for administrative purposes only, shall be located in the Department of Administration.

Done in Raleigh, North Carolina, this the 31st day of January in the year of our Lord, one thousand nine hundred eighty-five.

_____

James G. Martin, Governor
State of North Carolina

Code of Judicial Conduct
CANON 3
A Judge Should Perform the Duties of His Office Impartially and Diligently

The judicial duties of a judge take precedence over all his other activities. His judicial duties include all the duties of his office prescribed by law. In the performance of these duties, the following standards apply:

A. Adjudicative Responsibilities.

(1) A judge should be faithful to the law and maintain professional competence in it. He should be unswayed by partisan interests, public clamor, or fear of criticism.

. . . .

(4) A judge should accord to every person who is legally interested in a proceeding, or his lawyer, full right to be heard according to law, and, except as authorized by law, neither initiate nor consider *ex parte* or other communications concerning a pending or impending proceeding. A judge, however, may obtain the advice of a disinterested expert on the law applicable to a proceeding before him.

. . . .

(6) A judge should abstain from public comment about a pending or impending proceeding in any court, and should require similar abstention on the part of court personnel subject to his direction and control. This subsection does not prohibit judges from making public statements in the course of their official duties or from explaining for public information the procedures of the court.

. . . .

C. Disqualification.

(1) A judge should disqualify himself in a proceeding in which his impartiality might reasonably be questioned, including but not limited to instances where:

    (a) He has a personal bias or prejudice concerning a party, or personal knowledge of disputed evidentiary facts concerning the proceedings;

    (b) He served as lawyer in the matter in controversy, or a lawyer with whom he previously practiced law served during such association as a lawyer concerning the matter, or the judge or such lawyer has been a material witness concerning it;

(c) He knows that he, individually or as a fiduciary, or his spouse or minor child residing in his household, has a financial interest in the subject matter in controversy or in a party to the proceeding, or any other interest that could be substantially affected by the outcome of the proceeding;

(d) He or his spouse, or a person within the third degree of relationship to either of them, or the spouse of such a person:

(i) Is a party to the proceeding, or an officer, director, or trustee of a party;

(ii) Is acting as a lawyer in the proceeding;

(iii) Is known by the judge to have an interest that could be substantially affected by the outcome of the proceeding;

(iv) Is to the judge's knowledge likely to be a material witness in the proceeding.

(2) A judge should inform himself about his personal and fiduciary financial interests, and make a reasonable effort to inform himself about the personal financial interests of his spouse and minor children residing in his household.

(3) For the purposes of this section:

(a) The degree of relationship is calculated according to the civil law system;

(b) "Fiduciary" includes such relationships as executor, administrator, trustee, and guardian;

(c) "Financial interest" means ownership of a legal or equitable interest, however small, or a relationship as director, advisor, or other active participant in the affairs of a party, except that:

(i) Ownership in a mutual or common investment fund that hold securities is not a "financial interest" in such securities unless the judge participates in the management of the fund;

(ii) An office in an educational, religious, charitable, fraternal, or civic organization is not a "financial interest" in securities held by the organization;

(iii) The proprietary interest of a policyholder in a mutual insurance company, of a depositor in a mutual savings association, or a similar proprietary interest, is a "financial interest" in the organization only if the outcome of the proceeding could substantially affect the value of the interest;

(iv) Ownership of government securities is a "financial interest" in the issuer only if the outcome of the proceeding could substantially affect the value of the securities.

D. Remittal of Disqualification.

A judge disqualified by the terms of Canon 3C(1)(c) or Canon 3C(1)(d) may, instead of withdrawing from the proceeding, disclose on the record the basis of his disqualification. If, based on such disclosure, the parties and lawyers, independently of the judge's participation, all agree in writing that the judge's relationship is immaterial or that his financial interest is insubstantial, the judge is no longer disqualified, and may participate in the proceeding. The agreement, signed by all parties and lawyers, shall be incorporated in the record of the proceeding.

Local Codes

CITY OF CHARLOTTE CODE
ARTICLE III. CODE OF ETHICS FOR CITY OFFICIALS

Sec. 2-71. Declaration of policy.

(a) The proper operation of democratic government requires that public officials and employees be independent, impartial and responsible to the people; that governmental decisions and policy be made in proper channels of the governmental structure; that public office not be used for personal gain; and that the public have confidence in the integrity of its government.

(b) In recognition of these goals, a code of ethics for city officials is hereby adopted. The purpose of this article is to establish guidelines for ethical standards of conduct for all such officials by setting forth those acts or actions that are incompatible with the best interests of the city.

Sec. 2-72. Definitions.

As used in this article, the following terms shall have the meanings indicated:

Business entity means any business, proprietorship, firm, partnership, person in representative or fiduciary capacity, association, venture, trust or corporation which is organized for financial gain or for profit.

City official means the mayor, members of the city council, the city manager, assistant city manager and department heads.

Immediate household means the city official, his spouse and all dependent children of the city official.

Interest means direct or indirect pecuniary or material benefit accruing to a city official as a result of a contract or transaction which is or may be the subject of an official act or action by or with the city. For the purpose of this article a city official shall be deemed to have an interest in the affairs of:

(1) Any person in his immediate household, as such term is defined in this section;

(2) Any business entity in which the city official is an officer or director; or

(3) Any business entity in which in excess of five (5) percent of the stock of, or legal or beneficial ownership of, is controlled or owned directly or indirectly by the city official.

Official act or *action* means any legislative, administrative, appointive or discretionary act of any city official.

Sec. 2-73. Standards of conduct.

(a) *Scope.* All city officials as defined in this article shall be subject to and abide by the following standards of conduct.

(b) *Interest in contract or agreement.* No city official, as herein defined, shall have or thereafter acquire an interest in any contract or agreement with the city.

(c) *Use of official position.* No city official shall use his official position or the city's facilities for his private gain, nor shall he appear before or represent any private person, group or interest before any department, agency, commission or board of the city except in matters of purely civic or public concern. The provisions of this paragraph (c) are not intended to prohibit a city official's use of parking permits and are not intended to prohibit his speaking before neighborhood groups and other nonprofit organizations.

(d) *Disclosure of information.* No city official shall use or disclose confidential information gained in the course of or by reason of his official position for purposes of advancing:

(1) His financial or personal interest:

(2) A business entity of which he is an owner (in part or in whole), an officer or a director; or

(3) The financial or personal interest of a member of his immediate household or that of any other person.

(e) *Incompatible service.* No city official shall engage in, or accept private employment or render service for private interest, when such employment or service is incompatible with the proper discharge of his official duties or would tend to impair his independence of judgment or action in the performance of his official duties, unless otherwise permitted by law and unless disclosure is made as provided in this article.

(f) *Gifts.* No city official shall directly or indirectly solicit any gift, or accept or receive any gift having a value of fifty dollars ($50.00) or more, whether in the form of money, services, loan, travel, entertainment, hospitality, thing or promise, or any other form, under circumstances in which it could reasonably be inferred that the gift was intended to influence him, or could reasonably be expected to influence him, in the performance of his official duties, or was intended as a reward for any official action on his part. Legitimate political contributions shall not be considered as gifts under the provisions of this paragraph (f).

(g) *Special treatment.* No city official shall grant any special consideration, treatment or advantage to any citizen beyond that which is available to every other citizen.

Sec. 2-74. Disclosure of interest in legislative action.

The mayor or any member of the city council who has an interest in any official act or action before the council shall publicly disclose on the record of the council the nature and extent of such interest, and shall withdraw from any consideration of the matter if excused by the council pursuant to section 3.23(a) of the city charter.

Sec. 2-75. General disclosure; city clerk to prescribe form and fees for copying.

(a) All city officials, as herein defined, shall file with the city clerk on the first day of February of each year, a statement containing the following information:

(1) The identity, by name and address, of any business entity of which he or any member of his immediate household is an owner (as defined in section 2-72 of this chapter), officer or director. Additionally, the city official and spouse shall give the name of their employer or, if self-employed, state the nature of their work.

(2) The identity, by location and address, of all real property located in the county owned by the city official or any member of his immediate household, including an option to purchase, or lease for ten (10) years or more, other than his personal residence.

(b) The statements required by this section shall be filed on a form prescribed by the city clerk and are public records available for inspection and copying by any person during normal business hours. The city clerk is authorized to establish and charge reasonable fees for the copying of statements.

Sec. 2-76. Investigations instigated by city council; city manager; any other person.

(a) The city council may direct the city attorney to investigate any apparent violation of this article, as it applies to the mayor, any member of the city council, city manager or city clerk, and to report the findings of his investigation to the city council.

(b) The city manager may direct the city attorney to investigate any apparent violation of this article as it applies to assistant city managers and department heads, and to report the findings of his investigation to the city manager.

(c) The city council may direct the city manager to investigate any apparent violation of this article by the city attorney, and to report the findings of his investigations to the city council.

(d) Any person who believes that a violation of this article has occurred may file a complaint in writing with the city council when the mayor, a member of the city council, city manager, city clerk or city attorney is the subject of the complaint, or with the city manager when an assistant city manager or department head is the subject of the complaint, who may thereafter proceed as provided in paragraphs (a) through (c) of this section.

Sec. 2-77. Sanctions by city manager; city council; rights of accused at hearings.

(a) If the city manager, after the receipt of an investigation by the city attorney, has cause[d] to believe a violation of this article has occurred, he shall schedule a hearing on the matter. The city official who is charged with the violation shall have the right to present evidence, cross-examine witnesses, including the complainant or complainants, and be represented by counsel at the hearing. If, after such hearing and a review of all the evidence, the city manager finds that a violation of this article has occurred, he shall take whatever lawful disciplinary action he deems appropriate, including but not limited to, reprimand, suspension, demotion or termination of service.

(b) If the city council, after receipt of an investigation by the city attorney, has cause to believe a violation has occurred, the city council shall schedule a hearing on this matter. The official who is charged with the violation shall have the right to present evidence, cross-examine witnesses, including the complainant or complainants, and be represented by counsel at the hearing. If, upon the conclusion of the hearing, at least seven (7) members of the council vote to find a violation has occurred, the council may adopt a resolution of censure which shall be placed as a matter of record in the minutes of an official council meeting.

Sec. 2-78. Advisory opinions.

When any city official has a doubt as to the applicability of any provision of this article to a particular situation, or as to the definition of terms used in this article, he may apply to the city attorney for an advisory opinion. The city official shall have the opportunity to present his interpretation of the facts at issue and of the applicability of provisions of this article before such advisory opinion is made.

TOWN OF CHAPEL HILL
CHARTER

Sec. 3.12. Disclosure of property and business interests.

(a) The Town Council of Chapel Hill may require by ordinance the disclosure by the Mayor and members of the Council of their, and their spouses', personal financial interests including but not limited to interests in real property and in entities doing business with the town or applying for permits or approvals from the Town. The Council may establish minimum percentage interests below which disclosure would not be required.

(b) The Town Council of Chapel Hill may require by ordinance that the Mayor and Council members shall not vote on matters involving their property or business interests; provided, that the Council may exempt from disqualification matters such as zoning or development decisions in which all properties similarly situated would be similarly affected.

[Added to the Charter of the Town of Chapel Hill by Chapter 478, Section 4, of the 1989 Session Laws.]

CITY OF GREENSBORO
CODE OF ORDINANCES

Sec. 2-142. Private interest of members.

No member of any board or commission may discuss, advocate or vote on any matter in which he has a separate, private or monetary interest, either direct or indirect, and no member may discuss before the council or its committees any matter which has been, is, or will be considered by the board or commission on which he serves, and in which he has a separate, private or monetary interest, either direct or indirect. Any member who violates this provision may be subject to removal from the board or commission.

GUILFORD COUNTY CODE
DIVISION 2. FINANCIAL DISCLOSURE

Sec. 1-51. Nature and filing of disclosure.

Every member of the board of commissioners of Guilford County shall within thirty (30) days after the effective date of this act [this division] or within thirty (30) days after assuming office disclose any legal, equitable or beneficial interest he or his spouse may have in any real property in Guilford County which is in the zoning, water and sewer jurisdiction of the board of county commissioners of Guilford County.

This disclosure shall be filed in writing with the clerk of superior court and shall include all real property which any commission member holds title to, individually or jointly, any real property held in trust as well as any pecuniary interest he may have in any business, firm or corporation of whatever nature, which holds title to or has any ownership interest in any real property within the zoning, water and sewer jurisdiction of the board of commissioners of Guilford County.

Sec. 1-52. Interest in business, firm, etc., awarded county contracts.

Every member of the board of commissioners of Guilford County shall disclose any legal, equitable or beneficial ownership interest he may have in any business, firm or corporation, of whatever nature, which is doing business with Guilford County pursuant to contracts which have been awarded by the board of county commissioners.

Sec. 1-53. Ownership interest in business attempting to secure county contract.

Every member of the board of county commissioners of Guilford County shall disclose any legal, equitable or beneficial ownership interest he may have in any business, firm, or corporation, of whatever nature, which is attempting to secure the award of a bid from the county, prior to the award of any contract.

Sec. 1-54. Interest in real property; ownership in firm doing business with county.

The acquisition by any member subject to this act [this division] of any legal, equitable or beneficial interest in real property within the zoning, water and sewer jurisdiction of the board of commissioners of Guilford shall be disclosed within thirty (30) days after the acquisition of same. Any legal, equitable or beneficial ownership interest which any member has in any business, firm or corporation, of whatever nature, with whom Guilford County is now doing business, shall be disclosed within thirty (30) days after the effective date of this act [this division] or within thirty (30) days after acquisition of the ownership interest.

Sec. 1-55. Voting on matters involving ownership interest.

Every board member who has an ownership interest required to be disclosed by this act [this division] shall disqualify himself from voting on any matter involving any such ownership interest which comes for official action before the board of county commissioners of Guilford County.

Sec. 1-56. Penalties; forfeiture of office.

Any member who violates any provision of this act [this division] shall be guilty of a misdemeanor and may be fined not more than one thousand dollars ($1,000.00) or imprisoned not more than one year, or both. Any member who is convicted of a violation of any provision of this act [this division] shall forfeit his elected or appointed office, and such office shall be considered vacant as of the date of the final judgment of conviction.

ORANGE COUNTY CODE

Sec. 19. Every member of the Board of Commissioners of Orange County shall disclose any legal, equitable, beneficial or contractual interest he/she or his/her spouse may have in any real property in Orange County. The real property which must be disclosed includes all real property which any Board member or his/her spouse holds title to, individually or jointly, any real property held in trust as well as any pecuniary interest he/she may have in any business, firm, or corporation of whatever nature, which holds title to or has any ownership interest in any real property within Orange County. Such disclosure shall contain the general location of the real property, but need not include its value.

Sec. 20. Every member of the Board of Commissioners of Orange County shall disclose any legal, equitable, beneficial or contractual interest he/she may have in or with any business, firm, or corporation, of whatever nature, which is doing business with Orange County pursuant to contracts which have been awarded by Orange County.

Sec. 21. Every member of the Board of County Commissioners of Orange County shall disclose any legal, equitable, beneficial or contractual interest he/she may have in any business, firm, or corporation, of whatever nature, which is attempting to secure the award of a bid from Orange County or the approval of any Board or Agency of Orange County.

Sec. 22. The disclosures required in Sections 19, 20 and 21 shall be in writing and filed with the Clerk of Superior Court of Orange County and with the Clerk to the Board of Commissioners of Orange County.

Sec. 23. The written disclosures required in Sections 19, 20 and 21 shall be made within the following time periods which are applicable:
  (1) the later of 30 days after the effective date of this title or 30 days after the Board member has assumed office;
  (2) the earlier of 30 days of the acquisition of any legal, equitable, beneficial or contractual interest in the property or business, firm, or corporation required to be disclosed in Sections 19, 20 and 21 or prior to the award by Orange County of a contract with or a permit or other approval to a business, firm, or corporation required to be disclosed in Sections 20 and 21.

Sec. 24. Subject to the limitations contained in this section, every Board member who has an interest required to be disclosed by this title shall disqualify himself/herself from voting on any matter involving any such interest which comes for official action before the Board of County Commissioners of Orange County. The following interests do not require disqualification:

(1) interest in real property which must be disclosed in Section [19] provided the issue before the Board of Commissioners is one of policy that affects the real property disclosed no differently than all other property similarly situated.

(2) an interest in business, firm, or corporation which is negligible from the point of view of the operation of the business, firm, or corporation.

Sec. 25. Any member who violates any provision of this title shall be guilty of a misdemeanor and may be fined not more than one thousand dollars ($1,000) or imprisoned not more than one year, or both. Any member who is convicted of a wilful second violation of any provision of this act shall forfeit his/her elected or appointed office, and such office shall be considered vacant as of the date of the final judgment of conviction.

Sec. 26. This Title shall apply only to Orange County.

[Title added to the Orange County Code by Chapter 460 of the 1987 Session Laws. Section numbering is from that session law.]